At Issue

Policing the Internet

Other Books in the At Issue Series:

At Issue

I Policing the Internet

Roman Espejo, Book Editor

GREENHAVEN PRESS
A part of Gale, Cengage Learning

GALE
CENGAGE Learning·

Detroit • New York • San Francisco • New Haven, Conn • Waterville, Maine • London

GALE
CENGAGE Learning·

Elizabeth Des Chenes, *Director, Publishing Solutions*

© 2012 Greenhaven Press, a part of Gale, Cengage Learning

Gale and Greenhaven Press are registered trademarks used herein under license.

For more information, contact:
Greenhaven Press
27500 Drake Rd.
Farmington Hills, MI 48331-3535
Or you can visit our Internet site at gale.cengage.com

For product information and technology assistance, contact us at

Gale Customer Support, 1-800-877-4253
For permission to use material from this text or product, submit all requests online at
www.cengage.com/permissions

Further permissions questions can be emailed to permissionrequest@cengage.com

Articles in Greenhaven Press anthologies are often edited for length to meet page requirements. In addition, original titles of these works are changed to clearly present the main thesis and to explicitly indicate the author's opinion. Every effort is made to ensure that Greenhaven Press accurately reflects the original intent of the authors. Every effort has been made to trace the owners of copyrighted material.

Cover photograph reproduced by permission of Brand X Pictures.

LIBRARY OF CONGRESS CATALOGING-IN-PUBLICATION DATA

Policing the internet / Roman Espejo, book editor.
     p. cm. -- (At issue)
     Includes bibliographical references and index.
     ISBN 978-0-7377-5590-9 (hardcover) -- ISBN 978-0-7377-5591-6 (pbk.)
     1. Computer crimes--Prevention. 2. Internet--Law and legislation. 3. Internet--Social aspects. I. Espejo, Roman, 1977-
     HV6773.P65 2012
     364.16'8--dc23
                                                                2012001663

Printed in the United States of America
1 2 3 4 5   16 15 14 13 12
FD123

Contents

Introduction

According to the US Federal Trade Commission (FTC), phishing "involves Internet fraudsters who send spam or pop-up messages to lure personal information (credit card numbers, bank account information, Social Security number, passwords, or other sensitive information) from unsuspecting victims."[1] A business or organization familiar to the targeted user may request the confirmation, validation, or update of an account. "Some phishing emails threaten a dire consequence if you don't respond," the FTC warns. It is purported that the term was created in 1996 by hackers who stole names and passwords of America Online account holders, using fishing as an analogy: the "sea" is Internet users, and the "phish" is personal information. Phish also referred to hacked accounts, which phishers traded with each other.

In the early years of the World Wide Web, phishers sent text-based, often poorly written e-mails that could be easily identified as fake. But in 2003, their tactics became increasingly sophisticated, registering lookalike domain names such as "yahoo-billing.com" and "microsoft.checkinfo.com" to trick users. Phishers also incorporated stolen designs and logos from websites in their e-mails and spoofed the return addresses to seem as if they came from the impersonated companies. A year later, they began to use instant messaging via legitimate sites; programming to disguise fraudulent Internet addresses in users' address bars to appear authentic; and set up equally convincing false bank, online pharmacy, and loan agency sites to scam credit card information. In 2006, security software company Symantec claims to have encountered more than three-hundred thousand unique phishing e-mails and blocked them nearly three billion times.

1. www.ftc.gov, October 2006. http://www.ftc.gov/bcp/edu/pubs/consumer/alerts/alt127.shtm.

As phishers' scams evolve technologically, phishing is viewed as a growing threat among many Internet security professionals. "One thing that has become clear to us is that the profile of a typical phisher has changed," says Zulfikar Ramzan, a technical director and architect with Symantec.[2] "While the stereotypical phisher in the early days might have been the proverbial teenager in his mother's basement perpetrating mischief at two o'clock in the morning, today's phishers comprise fairly well organized business-oriented groups that are financially motivated," he insists. Security firm RSA reports that phishing attacks rose 27 percent in 2010 from the previous year to more than two-hundred thousand, including deceptive schemes that offered victims financial rewards. "American consumers were sent bogus IRS [Internal Revenue Service] notices, which claimed they would receive a tax refund after updating their online banking details," RSA observes.[3] "In another multi-targeted attack, online users were baited into entering their login credentials by an e-mail that masqueraded as a Coca-Cola customer satisfaction survey," the firm adds, alleging that the attack offered a cash prize for filling out the survey, which would be deposited in their bank accounts. Furthermore, Microsoft's *Security Intelligence Report* for May 2011 claimed that phishing attacks on social networking sites increased 1,200 percent, making up 84.5 percent of all phishing activities.

To others, however, the threat of phishing has been exaggerated. Applying several economic principles, Cormac Herley and Dinei Florêncio, researchers at Microsoft, argue that the online scam is largely unprofitable because phishers "share a finite resource" of income that "has a limited ability to regen-

2. Symantec Connect Community, June 29, 2009. http://www.symantec.com/connect/blogs/brief-history-phishing-part-i.
3. *RSA Monthly Online Fraud Report*, January 2011. http://www.rsa.com/solutions/consumer_authentication/intelreport/11244_Online_Fraud_report_0111.pdf.

erate" because as dollars are phished, they are no longer available. Briefly explaining their theory, Herley and Florêncio contend that

> The total revenue (all dollars stolen through phishing) is equal to the total cost (dollar value of the opportunity that phishers gave up in other occupations). The average revenue for a given phisher is the same (or slightly lower) than he would have made at another available occupation for his skill level. The easier phishing gets, the worse the economic picture for phishers. As phishers put more and more effort into the endeavor the total revenue falls rather than rises.[4]

Contrary to the get-rich-quick machinations of a mastermind hacker, they call phishing a "low skill, low reward business." Moreover, Herley and Florêncio are skeptical of the financial losses due to phishing and propose that victims lost $61 million in 2007 rather than the reported $3.2 billion.

Phishing is but one of the online perils that concern—and frequently divide—lawmakers, advocates, and experts. From cyberterrorism to cyberbullying, the authors in *At Issue: Policing the Internet* investigate and debate these and other issues. The wide-ranging, contrasting viewpoints presented in this volume underline the major arguments for and against regulation of and legal enforcement on the Internet.

---

4. "A Profitless Endeavor: Phishing as Tragedy of the Commons," 2008. http://research.microsoft.com/pubs/74159/NSPW08_final.pdf.

1

Teens Need Policing Online

Kate Fogarty

Kate Fogarty is an assistant professor in the Department of Family, Youth, and Community Services at the University of Florida's Institute of Food and Agricultural Sciences.

With access to the Internet at home, school, and on smart phones, teens are in danger of being solicited for sex or bullied online through social networks, text updates, blogs, and chat rooms. Online sexual solicitation of minors includes exposure to pornography, requests to discuss sex or perform a sexual act, and the disclosure of personal information. Cyberbullying involves the use of electronic communication to intimidate and harass—from exacting revenge to publicly sharing personal information. Parents must alert their children of these threats and enforce ground rules for Internet use. Additionally, awareness campaigns about online sexual solicitation and cyberbullying should be promoted in schools, and adults should collaborate with law enforcement agencies on Internet policing.

If you believe e-mail, blogs, text messaging, instant messaging, social networking sites, and 3-D virtual worlds (with avatars) are a completely harmless way for teens to communicate, think again! Most teens have Internet access at home, school and most everywhere with smart phones (cell phones with texting and Internet access), netbooks, and laptops. The Internet provides opportunities for private communication in

Kate Fogarty, "Teen Safety in Cyberspace," *Electronic Data Information Source*, University of Florida IFAS Extension, 2009, pp. 1–4. Copyright © 2009 University of Florida IFAS Extension. All rights reserved. Reproduced by permission.

the form of text updates, blogs, and chat rooms. These online communication aids are not themselves a problem, but the threat of being sexually solicited or bullied while online is a problem for teens.

While online, teens may be persuaded to do things that they do not want to, such as share private information, be sexually solicited, and/or experience public humiliation. Some worst-case scenarios—take, for example, Megan Meier, who committed suicide after being cyberbullied—got our attention and brought changes in the law and policy. However, adults' (youth staff and parents) skills in preventing cyberbullying and sexual solicitation are not where they need to be. This article will

- define online sexual solicitation and cyberbullying;

- explain the risk factors and negative effects of these communications; and

- outline effective ways to protect youth from harm.

Online Sexual Solicitation

Online sexual solicitation is a form of sexual harassment that occurs in cyberspace (in other words, in all electronic forms of communication such as the Internet and text messaging). Incidents of online sexual solicitation include exposure to pornography; being asked to discuss sex online and/or do something sexual; or requests to disclose personal information. This can start when an adult or peer initiates an online nonsexual relationship with a child or adolescent, builds trust, and seduces him into sexual acts.

Several studies have found that:

- 30% of teen girls who used the Internet frequently had been sexually harassed while they were in a chat room.

- 37% of teens (male and female) received links to sexually explicit content online.

- 30% of teens have talked about meeting someone they met online.

Online sexual solicitation can be a traumatic experience for victims. About 25% of youth who were sexually solicited felt "extremely afraid or upset" in response to the incident. Those most affected by sexual solicitation included teens that were:

- aged 10–13,

- solicited more aggressively online,

- sexually solicited on a computer in another person's home,

- currently struggling with major symptoms of depression.

About 25% of youth who were sexually solicited felt "extremely afraid or upset" in response to the incident.

There are several signs—traits, life circumstances, and actions—that parents and adults should be aware of in order to keep teens from online communication with sexual predators. Studies find that teens at the greatest risk for online sexual solicitation are:

- females between the ages of 13 and 17 years—in fact, 70% of teens who are sexually solicited are girls.

- teens who behave in risky ways online, including participating in cyberbullying, posting sexy photos of themselves, and discussing sex online with strangers.

- teens with major depressive symptoms and/or who have experienced negative life transitions (moving to a new neighborhood, a death or divorce in their family).

- teens that go online more frequently—four or more days a week at two or more hours a day.

Cyberbullying

Bullying, defined as aggression on a continual basis between peers where one has a power advantage over another, is common among children and adolescents. Cyberbullying involves using electronic communication for these ends:

- teach someone a lesson

- put others down

- play pranks

- share personal information publicly

- stalk someone

- commit other overt attacks upon a person

As is the case with online sexual solicitation, preteens are more likely to suffer psychologically from cyberbullying than older teens.

Teens who cyberbully may feel that cyberspace is an impersonal place to vent, and, therefore, consider it less harmful than face-to-face bullying. However, cyberbullying can be very destructive. Examples include middle school teens starting a poll with their classmates, casting online votes for the ugliest girl in the school or unsolicited videos or photos taken in a locker room are posted on YouTube or forwarded by media messaging. In addition, threats or hateful words travel easily through cyberspace in e-mails or cell phone messages (voice or text) from an unrecognized phone number. Ironically, most cyberbullying takes place within a teen's immediate social circle and those most likely to be victimized are highly active in social networking sites, blogs, and chat rooms.

About 25% of teens report being victims of cyberbullying, and over a third (35%) of teens reported feeling unaffected by it. Yet, the vast majority of victims reported feelings of:

- frustration,

- anger,

- sadness, and

- social anxiety.

In addition, as is the case with online sexual solicitation, preteens are more likely to suffer psychologically from cyberbullying than older teens.

Solutions: Ways to Keep Teens Safe

Families and communities (youth-serving organizations, schools) can provide important resources for protecting teens from cyber harm. In fact, a majority (64%) of teen students reported believing that adults in school would try to stop cyberbullying. Still, less than a third (30%) of students reported that if they knew about it happening that they would inform an adult about it. The following research-based tips can help encourage teens to talk with you about cyberbullying and sexual solicitation, as well as keep your teens from being victims or perpetrators.

Many police and sheriff departments have officers dedicated to monitoring the Internet for cyber predators and bullies.

At-Home/Personal Interaction with Youth

- Get access to "parental block" software that protects your child from exploring inappropriate websites. There are many options you can find by typing "free Internet blocking software" into a search engine (for example, Google).

- Keep computers with Internet access in a centralized location in the home, not in your child's bedroom and set limits on data access on your teen's cell phone.

- Check your child's computer and data use history. (Type in "Internet monitoring software for parents" on a search engine—some options are specifically geared toward monitoring your child's activity on social networking sites such as Facebook and Myspace).

- Negotiate rules with your teen on cell phone use with regard to text and media messaging, and online data access.

- Set a family Internet and data use policy. Define the ground rules for Internet use, such as scheduled times, permissible websites, and limitations on cyber communication with familiar peers or close friends.

- When setting cyberspace rules, consider how vulnerable your child might be to sexual solicitation and cyberbullying. Base your decision on his or her life circumstances as well as age and stage of development. For example, rules for Internet use for children should be more restrictive than those set for teens.

- Because they value privacy, be prepared to enforce set consequences when teens fail to observe a "family Internet policy" (for example, teens can be held responsible for fixing damages from computer viruses or paying for data minutes overages) and setting appropriate limits and fair consequences.

- Teach your child what cyberbullying is and give some specific examples of what to look for; help them learn to identify and interpret information shared or comments made by the predator. Kids will often think they are the only ones experiencing this and that they should be able to handle it.

- Educate your teen about potential dangers of cyber communication and sharing information. It is very easy for a predator to learn where the child lives and goes to school from only a little bit of information.

- Help teens to role-play effective ways to respond to sexual solicitation and cyberbullying.

- If an incident involving victimization of your teen occurs, reassure him or her that Internet access will not be forever discontinued, nor will their cell phone be confiscated, unless such measures are deemed temporarily necessary for their immediate safety.

In the Community

- Promote awareness campaigns in schools to influence policy, acceptable online "netiquette," and support programs for prevention of online sexual solicitation and cyberbullying.

- Collaborate with your local law enforcement agencies. Many police and sheriff departments have officers dedicated to monitoring the Internet for cyber predators and bullies. They can educate your children or group about what constitutes cyberbullying, what their rights are, and how to respond. Taking action will tell your child you care and you know how to help them resolve the situation. Children are likely to think that parents don't understand and therefore can't be of help.

- As adults, get educated on options available to teens in cyberspace and learn how to use them, too. Often, an older teen can serve as a resource to educate adults as well as younger teens and preteens on cyber use and safety. Encourage your teen to report incidents of online sexual solicitation or cyberbullying to adults, and reinforce their beliefs that appropriate action will be taken in response to the event.

- Encourage your teen to get involved in face-to-face activities as alternatives to interaction on the Internet. Youth who are vulnerable, lonely, and low on social skills are most likely candidates for excessive Internet use, increasing the risk for exposure to cyberbullying and online sexual solicitation.

Parents must be alert to the way their children use electronic communications.

2

The Dangers for Teens Online Are Exaggerated

Rahul Parikh

Based in the San Francisco Bay Area of California, Rahul Parikh is a pediatrician and writes the PopRx column for Salon.

Fears of online sexual predators, cyberbullying, sexting, and other perils of the Internet are overblown. Statistics on the "e-risks" young users face are unreliable and inaccurate, and the risks of the online harms teens face are similar to offline harms. For instance, the prevalence of cyberbullying is not epidemic, and most perpetrators are not anonymous to their victims. Furthermore, less than 10 percent of teens who are sexually solicited online are approached by adults; the majority are solicited by their peers. In reality, the Internet helps teens mature, providing them a platform for self-expression, connecting with others, and social and political activism.

In David Schwimmer's recent film "Trust," a teen girl falls for a boy she meets on the Internet. But when they agree to meet face to face, she discovers he's an adult man approaching middle age. By now, we can all see the horror that is coming: The young girl is raped by a pedophile, and her world collapses into a million little pieces.

"Trust" is the latest film to stir our deep desire to protect children from the evil that lurks on the Web. Practically speaking, that may mean taking away teens' cell phones, sitting beside them as they use the computer, or buying filtering software. It's understandable that—like television, movies and rock 'n' roll before it—the Internet has become a lightning rod for parental anxiety. And as a pediatrician, I can assure you doctors have been pulled into this debate about "e-risks," as I call them: Internet pedophilia, sexting, cyberbullying and, most recently, "Facebook depression" (more on that later). Parents worry about how their teen's use of the Web is affecting their health. Do they need a prescription sleep aid, or is all that late-night gaming making it hard to sleep? Do they have ADHD [attention deficit hyperactivity disorder], or do most kids IM [instant message] 50 people while they're doing their homework? The American Academy of Pediatrics [AAP] issued a report in March [2011] on the risks posed to youth on the Internet and how doctors like me should address the issue.

Research studies do not show an increase in overall sexual predation as a result of Internet use among young people.

Conflicting Statistics

Yet accurate numbers about how often teens are exposed to or affected by e-risks don't exist. You may, for example, learn that sexting is rare and that only 4 percent of teenagers have sent sexually explicit messages or images on their cell phones, but another survey may tell you the number is as high as 30 percent. Disparate numbers exist for other e-risks as well, mostly because these surveys have wildly variable definitions of what they're measuring (the more acts of cruelty you include under your description of "cyberbullying," the more likely you'll get a "yes" from your subjects) as well as the age range of subjects.

Sameer Hinduja is a professor of criminal justice at Florida Atlantic University, whose expertise is cyberbullying and other e-risks. His research suggests that about 20 percent of youth have been either victims or perpetrators of cyberbullying. "That's not a statistic we should ignore, but it's also not an epidemic either," he said. In a report to the FCC [Federal Communications Commission] written by researchers at Harvard [university], the authors noted that the prevalence of cyberbullying is similar to that of offline bullying. The report also notes that contrary to popular perception, cyberbullies are rarely anonymous. Most online bullying victims know their perpetrators, and half are in school with them. Perhaps the most important question to ask is whether kids who are bullied online are in any more danger than those bullied in the schoolyard. Hinduja believes they are not.

There are similar perception and reality discrepancies with online sexual predators. Barry Glassner, the president of Lewis and Clark University, is a sociologist whose expertise is media studies. In 2000, Glassner wrote a respected book called *The Culture of Fear*. In an updated version of the book released last year [2010], he looked at the well-publicized statistic that "1 in every 7 young people has been sexually solicited online," which came from a University of New Hampshire study seized upon by child advocates who spread it in the name of Internet safety. But Glassner points out that less than 10 percent of those solicitations were between adults and teens. In fact, almost half of cases were teens soliciting other teens. (In the rest of the cases, the ages were unknown.) That doesn't necessarily make it acceptable, but is it really that different from two teens passing notes during English class?

Online sexual predation, similarly, isn't that different from what happens away from the Web. Research studies do not show an increase in overall sexual predation as a result of Internet use among young people. The kids most at risk of online harms are the same as those at risk for offline harms—

victims of sexual or physical abuse, or children in unstable homes, for example. Finally, our schema of a "Trust"-like predator as an older man preying on a child distracts from the reality that most sexual solicitation of minors is done by other minors.

Next, we have concerns about the association between Internet use and mental illness. The most recent buzz term: "Facebook depression." If you Google that term you might be led to believe that letting a teen use Facebook or other social network is going to spark a clinical melancholy. Yet there's no evidence to support such a medical problem. Sensible reports about the story emphasize that excess time on social networks may just be a contemporary symptom of depression and not, as the terminology would suggest, that social media is the latest public health scourge.

If we don't rationally understand ... what's lost if we hide our children from the Web, then how can we responsibly address the problem?

Going Online Is Actually Good

All these parental panics run contrary to an idea that has much more in the way of expert consensus: that the Internet actually helps teens mature by allowing them to connect with others, learn and even advocate for a better world. Scholars for the Digital Youth Project at the MacArthur Foundation interviewed 800 kids and spent over 5,000 hours observing them in their online lives over a three-year period. The sum of that research: We should be thankful when kids go online, not afraid.

Most young people, they found, spent time online connecting with people they know (and not total strangers who could pose a danger). They gravitated to topics related to sports, religion, school and other local activities in their lives.

In contrast with the stereotype that teens waste time online, researchers saw them finding new ways to express themselves and pioneering new rules of social behavior through blogging, movie making and podcasting. They became more media savvy. Another survey found the Internet to be a great place for youthful social activism. Fifty-four percent of teens surveyed said they have joined an online community on a social network in support of a cause, and 34 percent said they had volunteered for a campaign, nonprofit organization or charity online. There's no better example of this than the "It Gets Better Project," supporting the right of gays and lesbians to feel safe at school and in their communities.

These points aren't meant to minimize real online dangers, and they don't necessarily prove that the benefits outweigh the risks. But it's critical to keep perspective (something the AAP clinical report does very well). As a parent and a physician, I understand our instincts can't help but gravitate toward the worst-case scenarios, like that in "Trust." On the other hand, if we don't rationally understand the breadth and scope of e-risks, or what's lost if we hide our children from the Web, then how can we responsibly address the problem?

It's more sensible to teach our kids to be good digital citizens instead of racing to protect them from every tweet, text and graffiti on their Facebook wall.

That question led me back to Sameer Hinduja. What, I asked him, are we supposed to do about minimizing e-risks and getting the most of the Web for our kids? He was enthusiastic about the recommendation that pediatricians address the issue with families. But on that issue, I'm less inclined to agree. Prevention is the best medicine, but if I had to add up all of the "preventive advice" I'm supposed to run through with parents and kids, a visit to the doctor would take hours instead of the 15–20 minutes patients usually get.

More importantly, I'm still not sure what to do with the information once I have it. If a teen tells me he is sexting, should I tell his parents? Should I call the police? Or do I, as some have suggested, treat it as harmless, healthy flirtation, or even a form of safe sex? Admissions of sexual activity by teens to their doctors are, under most circumstances, confidential and protected by law in California. There are ethical, medical-legal and regulatory landmines that we aren't even close to sorting out.

Hinduja agreed that, for now, there are no easy answers to minimizing e-risks in or out of the doctor's exam room. He and many other experts believe the best solution is to focus on education and prevention instead of draconian measures like constant monitoring of Internet activity, cutting kids off from the Web, or applying harsh laws to punish them for what may be digressions of youth. And while it might be tempting to install Internet filtering or blocking software, they certainly won't help control a teen's smart phone. The cat and mouse game between technology and teens often moves too quickly for software companies to keep up.

"Don't demonize Facebook or other sites, or kids will just tune you out," he said. "We need to get comfortable enough to teach young people to use the Web responsibly." Hinduja has also helped create a nonprofit, nonpartisian website that provides sensible information on e-risks for youth.

Ultimately, it's more sensible to teach our kids to be good digital citizens instead of racing to protect them from every tweet, text and graffiti on their Facebook wall. Good citizenship isn't a radical aspiration at all. In that sense, the Internet isn't the brave new world it's cracked up to be. Rather, with all of its opportunities, choices and risks, it's just an extension of the everyday world.

3

The Internet Should
Be Regulated

Lawrence E. Strickling

Lawrence E. Strickling is US Assistant Secretary of Commerce for Communications and Information and administrator of the National Telecommunications and Information Administration (NTIA).

Since the commercialization of the Internet in the 1990s, the government and policymakers have adopted a "leave the Internet alone" approach. Nonetheless, after years of unfettered economic growth and social innovation, issues of privacy, security, and copyright infringement online have yet to be effectively addressed; existing regulatory structures are outdated and overly political. The government's role need not be heavy-handed, but for the Internet to survive, it must preserve trust by ensuring the safety of private user information, protection of copyrighted content, security of networks, and integrity of Internet governance systems. These goals can be achieved through the collaborative efforts of government agencies, foreign governments, and key Internet constituencies.

The United States, and indeed all nations that depend on the Internet, face an increasingly urgent set of questions regarding the roles of the commercial sector, civil society, governments, and multi-stakeholder institutions in the very dynamic evolution of the Internet. I can think of no more ap-

Lawrence E. Strickling, "Remarks by Lawrence E. Strickling, Assistant Secretary of Commerce for Communications and Information," February 24, 2010. http://www.nta.doc.gov.

propriate place to discuss these issues than the Media Institute, given the vital role the Internet plays in advancing our Nation's First Amendment values, and the Institute's long tradition as a forum for exploring the nexus between the First Amendment and communications policy.

From the very first encounter between our Constitution and the Internet, courts have recognized the Internet as an unprecedented gift to the First Amendment. When the Supreme Court first considered the relationship between the Internet and freedom of speech, the Court recognized the Internet as a "never ending world-wide conversation." Since then, the conversation has only grown, but as we become more economically, socially, politically—and even emotionally—dependent on the Internet, we must continue to examine how best to ensure that this conversation can continue, can engage more and more people, and can be a platform for innovation in both public and private sectors of societies around the world.

The Internet as Ecosystem

The wide reach and central role that the Internet plays in our society has prompted many to refer to the Internet as an 'ecosystem.' I'd like to spend a little time examining just whether the ecosystem metaphor is a useful guide for policymakers. What lessons can we draw from this metaphor and which lessons should we avoid?

In the physical world, I associate the dynamics of a natural ecosystem with two important concepts: first, the presence of some set of biological laws such as natural selection, that second, leads to a balance or equilibrium state so that even when there is a disturbance these natural operations and laws bring the ecosystem back to a equilibrium state (maybe different than before, but an equilibrium).

Applying this concept to the online ecosystem could lead us to accept the idea that the Internet is self-regulating and there is some natural order that will always emerge no matter how the system may be disturbed. From this concept some argue that policymakers should just leave the Internet alone.

In fact, "leaving the Internet alone" has been the nation's Internet policy since the Internet was first commercialized in the mid-1990s. The primary government imperative then was just to get out of the way to encourage its growth. And the policy set forth in the Telecommunications Act of 1996 was: "to preserve the vibrant and competitive free market that presently exists for the Internet and other interactive computer services, unfettered by Federal or State regulation."

This was the right policy for the United States in the early stages of the Internet, and the right message to send to the rest of the world. But that was then and this is now.

It's now time to respond to all the social changes being driven by the growth of the Internet.

The Third Generation of Internet Policy Making

As we at NTIA [National Telecommunications and Information Administration] approach a wide range of Internet policy issues, we take the view that we are now in the third generation of Internet policy making. Here's how history looks to us.

1. *Internet Policy 1.0: transition to commercialization (1990–2000):* In the 1990s, let's call this period, Internet Policy 1.0, when the first commercial Internet service providers began providing commercial service and the World Wide Web was created, opportunities for innovation and investment "at the edges" of the network and in the last mile were drivers of growth. Innovation "at the edges" meant the development of exciting and novel applications that were often, literally, conceived in a garage. The guiding philosophy was: the more the better. The gov-

ernment imperative was to seek unrestrained growth of the Internet. It not only worked, but some of those very innovations continue to facilitate the Internet's vitality and growth.

2. *Internet Policy 2.0: from the garage to Main Street (2001–2009)*: After the turn of the century and for the last decade, the Internet experienced tremendous economic growth and social innovation. We call this period, Internet Policy 2.0. By one estimate, half the number of U.S. homes had Internet access within ten years after commercialization, and NTIA estimates that today, about 70 percent of U.S. households have Internet access. Despite this growth, policy issues emerged during this era which have not been effectively addressed:

   • Privacy: During this past decade, more and more personal data was being collected leading to a growing unease with the 'notice & choice' model. How many of us really read those privacy policies or just click away at the "Yes, I agree . . ." in order to get on with what you want to buy, read or post?

   • Security: Individual users and large enterprises found that they were required to devote more time and money to addressing security threats.

   • Copyright infringement: Over the last ten years, we've seen great innovation in the development of new business models, such as iTunes, but at the same time, we've also seen a surge in the piracy of intellectual property, and the negative impacts this disregard for copyright law has had on traditional content industries.

3. *Internet Policy 3.0*: It's now time to respond to all the social changes being driven by the growth of the Internet. We need Internet Policy 3.0. We enter this new de-

cade recognizing that we rely on the Internet for essential social purposes: health, energy efficiency, and education. It's also a general engine for economic and social innovation. We must take rules more seriously if we want full participation, but we must keep the need for flexibility in mind.

An Agglomeration of Human Actors

We have much higher expectations of the Internet today than we've had in the intervening years. The Internet, and particularly broadband Internet, is the central nervous system of our information economy and society, and can provide unprecedented opportunities to address our current challenges in health care, energy efficiency, education, and government openness.

It is important not only to preserve, but to enhance access to this open and dynamic medium that fosters unprecedented innovation and public participation. Going back to the 'ecosystem' metaphor, the Internet is not a natural park or wilderness area that should be left to nature. In fact, I don't think any of you in this room really believe that we should "leave the Internet alone."

The government's role need not be one of a heavy-handed regulator.

It's more accurate to describe the Internet as an agglomeration of human actors—it's a large and growing social organization. There are no natural laws to guide it—and there is most certainly no self-regulating equilibrium point because this cacophony of human actors participating in this organization demands that there be rules or laws created to protect our interests. That's human nature. For example:

- If you're a user, you want to know that you can make a transaction online without your credit card information falling into the wrong hands.

- If you're a content owner, you want to be allowed take action against users that infringe your copyright.

- If you are a small backbone provider, you want rules to govern peering relationships with large providers.

- If you're a large enterprise, you want your investment to protect against hacking and intrusion to be sound.

- If you are a network owner, you may be against Net Neutrality rules, but that does not mean there are not any rules, it just means the network owners get to create their own rules about whether and when to discriminate.

Despite the tremendous economic growth and social innovation that has occurred online over the past decade, policy tensions such as these have arisen and have not been effectively addressed. Given all the human actors involved in the Internet with all their competing interests, we have to ask, do governments have to be involved to sort out these interests so that the Internet will continue to thrive?

Not a Heavy-Handed Regulator

I say yes but just as emphatically, I say that the government's role need not be one of a heavy-handed regulator. There's little question that our existing regulatory structures are poorly equipped to deal with these issues. They are too slow, they are too backward looking, and they are too political to be effective.

But it concerns me that in the absence of some level of government involvement, we will lose the one thing that the Internet must have—not just to thrive, but to survive—the trust of all actors on the Internet.

- If users do not trust that their credit card numbers and private information are safe on the Internet, they won't use it.

- If content providers do not trust that their content will be protected, they will threaten to stop putting it online.

- If large enterprises don't have confidence that their network will not be breached over the Internet, they will disconnect their network and limit access to business partners and customers.

- If foreign governments do not trust the Internet governance systems, they will threaten to balkanize [meaning to break up into smaller, often hostile, units] the Domain Name System which will jeopardize the worldwide reach of the Internet. Those are just some examples but I think this issue of trust applies to every actor on the Internet.

How do we meet the security challenge posed by the global Internet which will require increased law enforcement and private sector technology innovation yet respect citizen privacy and protect civil liberties?

Preserving and Maintaining Trust on the Internet

A good place for policymakers to start as we define our role and what our actions should be is to preserve and maintain trust in the Internet. (Interestingly it's easier for government agencies to organize to prevent bad actions rather than nurture good ones. So we have the DOJ [Department of Justice] Antitrust division but we do not have an agency that is *for* trust).

At NTIA, we're not a regulatory agency, but as the principal advisor to the President on telecommunications and information policy, I think we have role to play in preserving and building trust on the Internet.

Our agenda [in 2010] is to refocus on the "I" in NTIA— Internet and information policy—and play the role of preserving and building trust and to balance out the policy tensions I mentioned earlier.

Let me list for you our initiatives for the year:

- Privacy policy. Here's the question: How can we enable the development of innovative new services and applications that will make intensive use of personal information but at same time protect users against harm and unwanted intrusion into their privacy? We are launching a series of listening sessions this spring with industry, advocates and academics in the field, and will follow up with a notice of inquiry and public outreach events.

- Child protection and Freedom of Expression: As more children go online, how do we ensure proper targeting of law enforcement resources against serious crime while remembering that most important line of defense against harmful content is the well-informed and engaged parent or teacher? Later this year, the Online Safety Technology Working Group, created by Congress and convened by NTIA, will issue a report on the state of the art in child protection strategies online.

- Cybersecurity: How do we meet the security challenge posed by the global Internet which will require increased law enforcement and private sector technology innovation yet respect citizen privacy and protect civil liberties? We're participating in a Commerce Department cybersecurity initiative that will address these is-

sues, particularly as they relate to improving the pre-
paredness of industry for cyber attacks.

- Copyright protection: How do we protect against illegal
  piracy of copyrighted works and intellectual property
  on the Internet while preserving the rights of users to
  access lawful content? NTIA and our sister agency at
  the Department of Commerce, the US Patent and
  Trademark Office, are beginning a comprehensive consultation process that will help the Administration develop a forward-looking set of policies to address online copyright infringement in a balanced, Internet-
  savvy manner.

- Internet Governance: In our role administering the
  Federal government's relationship with the Internet
  Corporation for Assigned Names and Numbers
  (ICANN), how do we ensure that ICANN serves the
  public interest and conducts its activities with the
  openness and transparency that the global Internet
  community demands? Last fall, NTIA and ICANN set
  forth a framework for technical coordination of the
  naming and numbering system and I am looking forward to soon participating in the first of the adminis-
  trative reviews to ensure that these commitments are
  carried out in full.

All of these efforts must involve collaboration—among
government agencies, foreign governments when appropriate,
and key Internet constituencies—commercial, academia, civil
society.

Our approach to answering these questions will be to engage the key constituencies and serve as a convener. NTIA is
looking for solutions to these issues through consultations to
advance the ball forward.

We will be flexible in terms of outcomes—the solutions
that emerge through our consultations may be recommenda-

tions for legislation or regulation, but if they result in individual actors accepting new processes, so much the better.

At the end of the day, all of these initiatives have as their goal to preserve and protect the trustworthiness of this extraordinary medium.

If we are successful, maybe we will change our name to the National Trust the Internet Administration.

Thank you.

4

The Government Should Not Regulate the Internet

Larry Downes

Larry Downes is an information technology consultant and author of Unleashing the Killer App *and* The Laws of Disruption.

The Internet has withstood government attempts at regulation with laws and legislation as a "disruptive technology," challenging basic assumptions and operating principles of enterprise and governance. For example, with the accelerated evolution of the Internet, laws and interventions become quickly outdated, which inadvertently hinder technological development and innovation. Also, because of its global scale, geographic regulation and national laws become incompatible, unenforceable, and difficult to follow. Therefore, the solution lies in self-regulation of the Internet, successfully invented in numerous online communities and through the growing power of consumers.

Summing up the history of lawlessness on the American frontier, [historian] Frederick Jackson Turner famously concluded in 1893: "A system of administration was not what the West demanded; it wanted land."

Our modern information frontier, known inelegantly (and inaccurately) as "the Internet," has likewise resisted efforts from governments to impose their provincial laws, local regulations, and moral disapproval disguised as legislation. Porn and gambling purveyors move their servers off-shore; political dissidents take advantage of anonymous relays and encryption; broadband providers hire Washington lawyers to challenge the Federal Communications Commission [FCC] in old-fashioned courts.

And thank goodness. While politicians and self-appointed consumer advocates opportunistically decry anarchy on the digital borderlands, those of us who reside there know it runs a hell of a lot better than anyplace else we've lived. Digital life has its own norms and values, enforced by efficient and effective engineering. As it was on the American frontier, those systems reflect the environmental realities of digital life. From simple reputation systems such as eBay's buyer-and-seller ratings to elaborate self-policing by the 12 million participants in online World of Warcraft games, Internet communities tend to invent their own unique "systems of administration."

A "Disruptive Technology"

Even if the Internet really does need saving, however, the most useful thing for traditional regulators to do would be nothing. That's largely because the Internet is the poster child for what Harvard [University]'s Clayton Christensen calls a "disruptive technology"—an innovation that upends the core assumptions and operating principles for enterprises that try to embrace it. In this case the enterprise is pretty much every aspect of human life, and the disruption is felt most acutely in basic ideas about how to govern.

By design, democratic governments innovate slowly, incrementally, and deliberatively. But when that approach is applied to an ecosystem that expands and evolves at accelerating speeds, laws aimed at controlling the technology or how it's used become quickly outdated. And that's just the best-case scenario. Often, instantly anachronistic regulations lead to unintended consequences, warping or even stunting the development of new applications and products that weren't even on the drawing boards when the legislating started.

The most profound mismatch is geographic. Even national laws fail to encompass the increasingly global scale of digital life, creating a patchwork of incompatible rules that nobody can follow, or that cannot be enforced. I live in a small town north of the Berkeley Hills, in California. Every month, the local newspaper publishes a police blotter of petty theft from unlocked cars or the occasional unneighborly dispute over tree-trimming. But lately there have been also a few reports of identity theft, Internet scams, or downloaded viruses that erased files. What can our part-time police force do about any of that?

The ongoing and seemingly endless fight over "net neutrality" is a good example of bad regulating. For those who have somehow missed this, the FCC has been promising for over a year to implement what it calls "prophylactic" rules to limit how U.S. ISPs [Internet service providers] can manage network traffic for consumers in the future. When the rules were finally voted on in late December [2010] the agency was obliged to carve out well over a dozen exceptions to its basic principle of a "neutral" Internet, recognizing that in the last 10 years the technology has evolved to optimize popular applications and resource-intensive content such as voice and video.

There are exceptions for content-delivery networks, IP-based television and voice, and peering arrangements between backbone providers; special rules for nascent and resource-constrained mobile Internet users; and exemptions for e-book readers, game platforms, and coffee shops that offer limited forms of Internet access. The Internet has evolved into a much more complicated place than it was in 1998, when the FCC last paid it much attention.

For some, these caveats fatally undermine the goal of the rules, which was to ensure a "level playing field" for new participants in the Internet ecosystem. But these exceptions are crucial to maintain today's vastly expanded and improved online experience. The problem, rather, is that by putting an arbitrary stake in the ground, the FCC's "these but no more" exceptions will unintentionally slow or even smother further improvements in network-management techniques yet to be invented.

Given the rapid transition to mobile computing in progress, and the government-created problems of misallocated radio-spectrum and transmission-tower-siting limits for cellular carriers, the new rules could in particular upend the best engine of innovation the struggling economy currently has.

The agency promises to review its rule in two years. But two years in Internet time is an eternity.

I have faith that consumers, users, and citizens increasingly have the tools to make their views known and effect change when necessary—quickly and effectively.

Users Must Police Digital Life

Let me give an example, on the other hand, of good lawmaking. In 1996, Congress granted all Internet service providers—a term broadly defined—immunity from most forms of secondary liability, including state defamation laws, for content posted by users and other third parties. Blog hosts, broadband providers, and news sites that allow comments are not legally responsible for what their users say. Neither are companies such as Yelp, Twitter, YouTube, and Facebook, whose entire business relies on content shared by users.

Few other countries had the foresight to create this kind of "law-free" zone for innovators to play around in. As a result, the vast majority of social networking and other "Web 2.0" companies that led the second great wave of Internet innovation have their origins—and their headquarters—in the United States. It wasn't that U.S. lawmakers planned for Facebook and Twitter or could have if they wanted to. But by protecting startups from potentially lethal nuisance lawsuits, new applications were able to evolve on their own terms.

If governments do more harm than good, who's left to police digital life? The answer is the users themselves. One important side effect of social networking, user video, and app-based interactions has been the empowerment of consumers. Pro-regulatory advocates worry about what giant content providers such as Google or access companies including Verizon and Comcast might do in a future absent government intervention. But I have faith that consumers, users, and citizens increasingly have the tools to make their views known and effect change when necessary—quickly and effectively.

Facebook learns that lesson every time it tries to change how it manages user data, ironically falling victim to the very tools the company provides its users. Two years ago, a Facebook group called "People against the new Terms of Service" signed up 100,000 members in a matter of minutes. That's the starting point. Increasingly, users will overcome the traditionally high costs of collective action and exert their will as equals to corporations and governments that take technology in directions they don't like.

Early on, unfortunately, we may also have to endure episodes of digital mob rule, with all the negative consequences that go with it. That, too, is what happened in the American West. But over time, the posse and the hanging tree gave way to local sheriffs and circuit-riding judges. The frontier civilized itself.

The Internet will do the same. Only faster.

5

Cyberterrorism Is a Serious Threat

Kelly A. Gable

Kelly A. Gable is an adjunct professor of public international law at Drexel University Earle Mack School of Law.

The threat of crippling acts of cyberterrorism on the United States and other nations is real. Small-scale attacks on domestic power grids, telecommunications networks, and the financial services industry demonstrate the vulnerability of critical infrastructures. Hackers attempt to crack government and national defense computers thousands of times each day. Cyberterrorist activity has resulted in disruptive assaults on American and Korean government websites as well as a massive attack on major government, financial, and media websites in Estonia. National governments and international organizations must continue to take concerted steps to prevent and deter cyberterrorism, or else national and international security will be compromised.

It is a cold December day, already dark, when Aidan Smith leaves his office to catch the train home. As he is leaving the building, the power suddenly cuts out, bringing the elevator he is in to a screeching halt on the ground floor. He presses the emergency button, and the doors open, begrudgingly, to let him out. Shaken, he heads for the train station. As he steps out into the street, he realizes it is much darker than usual—

Kelly A. Gable, "Cyber-Apocalypse Now: Securing the Internet Against Cyberterrorism and Using Universal Jurisdiction As a Deterrent," *Vanderbilt Journal of Transnational Law*, vol. 43.57, 2010, pp. 59–66. Copyright © 2010 Vanderbilt University Law School. All rights reserved. Reproduced by permission.

every building, every street light, every stoplight is dark. Only the headlights from passing cars light the sidewalk as he slowly makes his way to the train station. He finally arrives, but finds that the station is barely lit and is jammed with people waiting for trains that are not coming. Checking the news on his BlackBerry, he sees that Washington, D.C., New York, Chicago, and Los Angeles have simultaneously lost all electricity and that Al Qaeda replaced the White House website with a message proclaiming that they have hacked into and shut down these major power grids to cripple the U.S. economy, as the stock markets, airports, and banks cannot function without electricity. In short, Al Qaeda has caused a cyber-apocalypse.

In a single day in 2008 . . . hackers targeted the Pentagon with six million attempts to access its computer system.

Although this situation is hypothetical, the possibility is disturbingly real. Hackers scan U.S. government computer systems literally thousands of times a day, looking for a way in. In 2001, hackers successfully attacked an electric power grid in California and a seaport in Houston; more recently, hackers planted malicious software in the U.S. power grid, oil and gas distribution computer systems, telecommunications networks, and computer systems of the financial services industry. In March 2007, researchers at the Department of Energy's Idaho National Laboratory caused a generator to self-destruct, just to see if they could. Although these attacks were narrower in scope and magnitude than the hypothetical scenario, they each demonstrate the vulnerability of critical U.S. infrastructure. The fact that each of these critical infrastructure systems is accessible via the Internet heightens (and arguably creates) this vulnerability.

Revolutionizing Terrorism

The Internet has revolutionized and exponentially increased the threat that terrorism poses to national and international security. The Internet not only makes it easier for terrorists to communicate, organize terrorist cells, share information, plan attacks, and recruit others, but also is increasingly being used to commit cyberterrorist acts. In February 2009, the Director of National Intelligence testified before the Senate Select Committee on Intelligence that terrorist groups have expressed their intent to use cyber attacks against the United States. Indeed, cyberterrorists and hackers attempt to penetrate Department of Defense computer systems thousands of times a day.

Cyberterrorism has become one of the most significant threats to the national and international security of the modern state, and cyberattacks are occurring with increased frequency. Starting on July 4, 2009, a week-long cyberattack crippled numerous U.S. and South Korean websites, including those of the U.S. Departments of Transportation and Treasury; the U.S. Federal Trade Commission; the South Korean President's Office; the South Korean National Assembly; and U.S. Forces Korea. Although the South Korean government initially believed that North Korea had perpetrated the attack, security experts later suggested that cyberterrorists operating in the United Kingdom may have been the source of the attack, which affected hundreds of thousands of personal computers across dozens of countries.

Estonia was the target of a comparably massive attack from April to May 2007, when a multi-week wave of cyberattacks effectively shut down the country by disrupting the websites of the Estonian President and Parliament, the vast majority of Estonian ministries, three of the country's six largest news organizations, and two of its major banks. The attack on Estonia was so effective partly because Estonia has established an "e-government," conducting most of its basic governmental operations via the Internet. For example, Estonians conduct more than 98% of their banking online, pay their taxes online, and vote online. Accordingly, these relatively simple attacks effectively brought the country to a halt for three weeks.

Other significant examples of cyberterrorism in the past few years include the theft of information regarding the new U.S. military stealth fighter jet, the hacking into the U.S. Air Force's air traffic control systems, and Titan Rain, which is the codename given by the U.S. government to a series of intelligence-gathering cyberattacks conducted by a group of Chinese hackers. Furthermore, these are only the most publicized of examples—every day cyberterrorists attempt to undermine national and international security and wreak havoc in order to further their terrorist agendas. In a single day in 2008, for instance, hackers targeted the Pentagon with six million attempts to access its computer system.

These attacks showcase a range of potential tools in the cyberterrorist's arsenal. Some may be relatively simple and low-tech; this also means they are relatively easy to deploy. They also highlight the potential damage that could be caused by more sophisticated attacks. In fact, cybersecurity has become so important that traditionally secretive organizations charged with protecting national security are speaking out about the threat. Increasingly, it is clear that the international community may only ignore cyberterrorism at its peril.

Cyberterrorism Defined

Roughly defined, cyberterrorism refers to efforts by terrorists to use the Internet to hijack computer systems, bring down the international financial system, or commit analogous terrorist actions in cyberspace. The United States has defined cyberterrorism as "a criminal act conducted with computers and resulting in violence, destruction, or death of its targets in an effort to produce terror with the purpose of coercing a government to alter its policies," and it includes attacks on computer networks and transmission lines within that definition. Put simply, cyberterrorism generally is understood as any terrorist act conducted in or by means of cyberspace or the Internet. This definition is necessarily broad and includes everything from basic hacking and denial of service attacks to concerted efforts to unleash weapons of mass distraction or mass disruption. Such a definition, however, is limited in application regarding the actor or actors and the intent behind the attack.

First, the term cyberterrorism refers only to terrorist actions taken by individuals, groups of individuals, or organizations such as Al Qaeda. To the extent that either a state or its agent was to act in similar ways, it would be considered an act of aggression or use of force under international law, which may be considered cyberwarfare.

Second, the term cyberterrorism refers only to those actions that are taken by terrorists with the intent or goal of causing destruction or inciting terror, generally for religious or political purposes, although financial gain to facilitate further attacks may be a secondary motivation. It often is difficult to distinguish cybercrime from cyberterrorism during an attack, as the key distinction lies in the intent behind the attack. Depending on his or her goal, a hacker could just as easily be a cyberterrorist as a cybercriminal.

> *Without a complete overhaul (or at least a significant retrofit) of the very structure of the Internet, these legal, policy, and technological methods will serve only to mitigate the potential effects of cyberterrorism.*

The primary security threat posed by the Internet involves the TCP/IP [Transmission Control Protocol/Internet Protocol] Protocol, the technology underlying the structure of the Internet and other similar networks. This underlying structure enables cyberterrorists to hack into one system and use it as a springboard for jumping onto any other network that is also based on the TCP/IP Protocol. Other threats to national and international security include direct attacks on the Internet and the use of the Internet as a free source of hacking tools.

These threats are not easy to eradicate. One problem underlying the widespread use of the Internet is the concept of irreversible dependence on technology: once the benefits of technologies like the Internet are realized, it is impossible not to use them. The technologies become an indispensable crutch for those determining policy strategies, both for foreign policy determinations and daily governmental operations.

Prevention and Deterrence Efforts

The cyberattacks on the Estonian, U.S., and South Korean governments, as well as the long list of similar attacks that came before them, have brought the issue of cyberterrorism prevention squarely before national governments and international organizations such as NATO [North Atlantic Treaty Organization], the Organization for Security and Cooperation in Europe (OSCE), the European Union, the United Nations, and the Council of Europe. These institutions are beginning to take steps to improve international cooperation to combat cyberterrorism. The OSCE recently established the Action Against Terrorism Unit. Similarly, NATO established a Cooperative Cyber Defense Center of Excellence in Estonia. The European Union also recently launched the Critical Information Infrastructure Protection Initiative. The United Nations Security Council and General Assembly have enacted resolutions to address terrorism or cyberterrorism. Possibly the most significant enactment is the Council of Europe's enactment of the Convention on Cybercrime, which is the first multilateral convention to address cybercrime.

These domestic and international organizations have made significant progress merely by taking these preliminary steps, but more must be done. The international community must recognize that, as a result of the fundamental insecurities inherent in the architecture of the Internet, none of these actions will prevent cyberterrorism completely. Without a complete overhaul (or at least a significant retrofit) of the very structure of the Internet, these legal, policy, and technological methods will serve only to mitigate the potential effects of cyberterrorism.

In the absence of feasible prevention, deterrence of cyberterrorism may be the best alternative. A longstanding concept of international law—universal jurisdiction—is one way to deter cyberterrorism. The likely effect can be seen by drawing analogies to other international crimes for which universal jurisdiction is recognized and by applying various rationales for universal jurisdiction. The borderless and transnational nature of the Internet and cyberterrorism complicates the application of territorial jurisdiction. The asynchronous pairing of territorial jurisdiction and borderless cyberterrorism means that territorial jurisdiction likely would be a less effective deterrent than universal jurisdiction. Without, at a minimum, a concerted effort at deterrence, cyberterrorism will continue to threaten national and international security.

6

Cyberterrorism Is Not a Serious Threat

Jerry Brito and Tate Watkins

Jerry Brito is a senior research fellow at George Mason University's Mercatus Center and director of its Technology Policy Program. Tate Watkins is a research associate at the Mercatus Center.

In recent years, dozen of bills related to cyberterrorism have inundated Congress. However, evidence for cyber attacks on government agencies and the nation's infrastructures is largely unsubstantiated. The real harm lies in the rise of a "cybersecurity industrial complex," which would be costly and have serious consequences. Regulatory measures would lead to intrusive government control of information on the Internet, threatening free speech and anonymity. Unproven warnings of cyberterrorism are inflammatory, and impending cybersecurity legislation would increase wasteful spending. Policymakers must stop the alarmist rhetoric, declassify evidence of cyberterrorist activity for more transparency, and separate unrelated dangers from the label of cyberterrorism.

In the last two years, approximately 50 cybersecurity-related bills have been introduced in Congress. In May [2011] the White House released its own cybersecurity legislative proposal. The Federal Communications Commission [FCC] and the Commerce Department have each proposed cybersecurity regulations of their own. Last year, Senate Armed Services Committee Chairman Carl Levin (D-Mich.) even declared that cyberattacks might approach "weapons of mass destruction in their effects." A rough Beltway consensus has emerged that the United States is facing a grave and immediate threat that can only be addressed by more public spending and tighter controls on private network security practices.

But there is little clear, publicly verified evidence that cyber attacks are a serious threat. What we are witnessing may be a different sort of danger: the rise of a cybersecurity-industrial complex, much like the military-industrial complex of the Cold War, that not only produces expensive weapons to combat the alleged menace but whips up demand for its services by wildly exaggerating our vulnerability.

The Regulatory Urge

The proposals on the table run the gamut from simple requests for more research funding to serious interventions in the business practices of online infrastructure providers. The advocates of these plans rarely consider their costs or consequences.

At one end of the spectrum, there have been calls to scrap the Internet as we know it. In a 2010 *Washington Post* op-ed, Mike McConnell, former National Security Agency chief and current Booz Allen Hamilton vice president, suggested that "we need to reengineer the Internet to make attribution, geolocation, intelligence analysis and impact assessment—who did it, from where, why and what was the result—more manageable." Former presidential cybersecurity adviser Richard Clarke has recommended the same. "Instead of spending money on security solutions," he said at a London security conference last year, "maybe we need to seriously think of redesigning network architecture, giving money for research into the next protocols, maybe even think about another, more secure Internet."

A re-engineered, more secure Internet is likely to be a very different Internet than the open, innovative network we know today. A government that controls information flows is a government that will attack anonymity and constrict free speech. After all, the ability to attribute malicious behavior to individuals would require users to identify themselves (or be identifiable to authorities) when logging on. And a capability to track and attribute malicious activities could just as easily be employed to track and control any other type of activity.

Many current and former officials, from Clarke to FBI [Federal Bureau of Investigation] Director Robert Mueller, have proposed requiring private networks to engage in deep packet inspection of Internet traffic, the online equivalent of screening passengers' luggage, to filter out malicious data and flag suspicious activity. The federal government already engages in deep packet inspection on its own networks through the Department of Homeland Security's "Einstein" program. Mandating the same type of monitoring by the Internet's private backbone operators—essentially giving them not just a license but a directive to eavesdrop—would jeopardize user privacy.

There have also been proposals at the FCC and in Congress for the certification or licensing of network security professionals, as well as calls for mandating security standards. While certification may seem harmless, occupational licensing mandates should never be taken lightly; they routinely restrict entry, reduce competition, and hamper innovation. Politicians have also called for substantial new government subsidies, including the creation of regional cybersecurity centers across the country to help medium-sized businesses protect their networks.

Many of the bills would mandate a new cybersecurity bureaucracy within either the Department of Homeland Security or the Defense Department. Many would also create new reporting requirements. For example, the administration's proposed legislation requires that private firms deemed by the head of Homeland Security to be "critical infrastructure" must develop cybersecurity plans and have those plans audited by federally accredited third parties.

With proposals as intrusive and expensive as these, you might think the case for federal intervention is overwhelming. But it isn't. Again and again, the regulators' argument boils down to "trust us."

Neither the probing of Pentagon computers nor the cited cases of cyberespionage . . . have any bearing on the probability of a successful attack on the electrical grid.

The CSIS Commission

One of the most widely cited arguments for more federal involvement in online security was made by the Commission on Cybersecurity for the 44th Presidency, which unveiled its report in December 2008. The commission, assembled by the Center for Strategic and International Studies (CSIS), a foreign policy think tank, in February 2008, served as a sort of cybersecurity transition team whoever the new president turned out to be. It was chaired by two members of Congress and composed of security consultants, academics, former government officials, and representatives of the information technology industry. Their report concluded that "cybersecurity is now a major national security problem for the United States" and urged the feds to "regulate cyberspace" by enforcing security standards for private networks.

Yet the commission offers little evidence to support those conclusions. There is a brief discussion of cyberespionage attacks on government computer systems, but the report does not explain how these particular breaches demonstrate a national security crisis, let alone one that "we are losing."

The report notes, for example, that Defense Department computers are "probed hundreds of thousands of times each day." Yet it fails to mention that probing and scanning networks are the digital equivalent of trying doorknobs to see if they are unlocked—a maneuver available to even the most unsophisticated would-be hackers. The number of times a computer network is probed is not evidence of a breach, an attack, or even a problem.

More ominously, the report warns: "Porous information systems have allowed opponents to map our vulnerabilities and plan their attacks. Depriving Americans of electricity, communications, and financial services may not be enough to provide the margin of victory in a conflict, but it could damage our ability to respond and our will to resist. We should expect that exploiting vulnerabilities in cyber infrastructure will be part of any future conflict."

An enemy able to take down our electric, communications, and financial networks at will would indeed be a serious threat. And it may well be the case that the state of security in government and private networks is deplorable. But the CSIS report cites no reviewable evidence to substantiate this supposed danger. There is no support for the claim that opponents have "mapped vulnerabilities" and "planned attacks." Neither the probing of Pentagon computers nor the cited cases of cyberespionage—for instance, the hacking of a secretary of defense's unclassified email—have any bearing on the probability of a successful attack on the electrical grid.

Nevertheless, the commission concludes that tighter regulation is the only way toward greater security. It is "undeniable," the report claims, that "market forces alone will never provide the level of security necessary to achieve national security objectives." But without any verifiable evidence of a threat, how are we to know what exactly the "appropriate level of cybersecurity" is and whether market forces are providing it? With at least some security threats, such as industrial espionage and sabotage, private industry has a strong incentive to protect itself. If there is a market failure here, the burden of proof is on those who favor regulation. So far they have not delivered.

Although they never explicitly say so, the report's authors imply that they are working from classified sources, which might explain the dearth of reviewable evidence. To its credit, the commission laments what it considers the "overclassification" of information related to cybersecurity. But this excessive secrecy should not serve as an excuse. If the buildup to the Iraq war teaches us anything, it is that we cannot accept the word of government officials with access to classified information as the sole evidence for the existence or scope of a threat.

Cyberwar: The Book

If the CSIS report is the document cyberhawks cite most, the most widely read brief for their perspective is the 2010 bestseller *Cyber War*, by Richard Clarke and Robert Knake, a cybersecurity specialist at the Council on Foreign Relations. This book makes the case that U.S. infrastructure is extremely vulnerable to cyber attack by enemy states. Recommendations include increased regulation of electrical utilities and Internet service providers.

"Obviously, we have not had a full-scale cyber war yet," Clarke and Knake write, "but we have a good idea what it would look like if we were on the receiving end." The picture they paint includes the collapse of the government's classified and unclassified networks, the release of "lethal clouds of chlorine gas" from chemical plants, refinery fires and explosions across the country, midair collision of 737s, train derailments, the destruction of major financial computer networks, suburban gas pipeline explosions, a nationwide power blackout, and satellites in space spinning out of control. In this world, they warn, "Several thousand Americans have already died, multiples of that number are injured and trying to get to hospitals. . . . In the days ahead, cities will run out of food because of the train-system failures and the jumbling of data at trucking and distribution centers. Power will not come back up because nuclear plants have gone into secure lockdown and many conventional plants have had their generators permanently damaged. High-tension transmission lines on several key routes have caught fire and melted. Unable to get cash from ATMs or bank branches, some Americans will begin to loot stores." All of which could be the result of an attack launched "in fifteen minutes, without a single terrorist or soldier appearing in this country."

Clarke and Knake assure us that "these are not hypotheticals." But the only verifiable evidence they present relates to several well-known distributed denial of service (DDOS) attacks. A DDOS attack works by flooding a server on the Internet with more requests than it can handle, thereby causing it to malfunction. A person carrying out a DDOS attack will almost certainly produce this flood of requests with a botnet—a network of computers that have been compromised without their users' knowledge, usually through a virus. Vint Cerf, one of the fathers of the Internet and Google's chief Net evangelist, has estimated that possibly a quarter of personal computers in use today are compromised and placed in unwilling service of a botnet.

Clarke and Knake cite several well-known DDOS attacks, such as the attacks on Estonia in 2007 and Georgia in 2008, both widely suspected to have been coordinated by Russia. They also mention an attack on U.S. and NATO [North Atlantic Treaty Organization] websites in 1999 after American bombs fell on the Chinese embassy in Belgrade. And they cite a July 4, 2009, attack on American and South Korean websites, widely attributed to North Korea. These reputedly state-sponsored operations, along with the hundreds of thousands of other DDOS attacks each year by private vandals, are certainly a sign of how vulnerable publicly accessible servers can be. They are not, however, evidence of the capability necessary to derail trains, release chlorine gas, or bring down the power grid.

The authors admit that a DDOS attack is often little more than a nuisance. The 1999 attack saw websites temporarily taken down or defaced, but it "did little damage to U.S. military or government operations." Similarly, the 2009 attacks against the United States and South Korea caused several government agency websites, as well as the websites of the NASDAQ Stock Market, the New York Stock Exchange, and *The Washington Post*, to be intermittently inaccessible for a few hours. But they did not threaten the integrity of those institutions. In fact, the White House's servers were able to deflect the attack easily thanks to the simple technique of "edge caching," which involves serving Web content from multiple sources, in many cases servers geographically close to users.

Without any formal regulation mandating that it be done, the affected agencies and businesses worked with Internet service providers to filter out the attacks. Once the attackers realized they were no longer having an effect, the vandalism stopped. Georgia, hardly the world's richest or most technologically sophisticated country, similarly addressed attacks on its websites by moving them to more resilient servers hosted outside of its borders.

Washington is filled with people who have a vested interest in conflating and inflating the threats to our digital security.

Clarke and Knake recognize that DDOS is a "primitive" form of attack that would not pose a major threat to national security. Yet DDOS attacks make up the bulk of the evidence for the dire threat they depict. If we have no verifiable evidence of the danger we're in, they write, it is merely because the "attackers did not want to reveal their more sophisticated capabilities, yet." With regard to the Georgian and Estonian episodes, they argue that the "Russians are probably saving their best cyber weapons for when they really need them, in a conflict in which NATO and the United States are involved."

When Clarke and Knake venture beyond DDOS attacks, their examples are easily debunked. To show that the electrical grid is vulnerable, for example, they suggest that the Northeast power blackout of 2003 was caused in part by the "Slammer" worm, which had been spreading across the Internet around that time. But the 2004 final report of the joint U.S.-Canadian task force that investigated the blackout explained clearly that no virus, worm, or other malicious software contributed to the power failure. Clarke and Knake also point to a 2007 blackout in Brazil, which they believe was the result of criminal hacking of the power system. Yet separate investigations by the utility company involved, Brazil's independent systems operator, and the energy regulator all concluded that the power failure was the result of soot and dust deposits on the high-voltage insulators on transmission lines.

Before we pursue the regulations that Clarke and Knake advocate, we should demand more precise evidence of the threat they portray and the probability that it will materialize. That will require declassification and a more candid, on-the-record discussion. . . .

The Cybersecurity-Industrial Complex

Washington is filled with people who have a vested interest in conflating and inflating the threats to our digital security. In his famous farewell address to the nation in 1961, President Dwight Eisenhower warned against the dangers of what he called the "military-industrial complex": an excessively close nexus between the Pentagon, defense contractors, and elected officials that could lead to unnecessary expansion of the armed forces, superfluous military spending, and a breakdown of checks and balances within the policy making process. Eisenhower's speech proved prescient.

Cybersecurity is a big and booming industry. The U.S. government is expected to spend $10.5 billion a year on information security by 2015, and analysts have estimated the worldwide market to be as much as $140 billion a year. The Defense Department has said it is seeking more than $3.2 billion in cybersecurity funding for 2012.

Traditional defense contractors, both to hedge against hardware cutbacks and get in on the ground floor of a booming new sector, have been emphasizing cybersecurity in their competition for government business. Lockheed Martin, Boeing, L-3 Communications, SAIC, and BAE Systems have all launched cybersecurity divisions in recent years. Other defense contractors, such as Northrop Grumman, Raytheon, and ManTech International, have also invested in information security products and services.

Traditional I.T. [information technology] firms such as McAfee and Symantec also see more opportunities to profit from cybersecurity business in both the public and private sectors. As one I.T. market analyst put it in a 2010 Bloomberg report: "It's a cyber war and we're fighting it. In order to fight it, you need to spend more money, and some of the core beneficiaries of that trend will be the security software companies." I.T. lobbyists, too, have pushed hard for cybersecurity budget increases. Nir Zuk, chief technology officer at Palo Alto Networks, complained to *The Register* last year that "money gets spent on the vendors who spend millions lobbying Congress."

Meanwhile, politicians have taken notice of the opportunity to bring more federal dollars to their states and districts. Recently, for example, the Air Force established Cyber Command, a new unit in charge of the military's offensive and defensive cyber capabilities. Cyber Command allows the military to protect its critical networks and coordinate its cyber capabilities, an important function. But the pork feeding frenzy that it touched off offers a useful example of what could happen if legislators or regulators mandate similar buildups for private networks.

Beginning in early 2008, towns across the country sought to lure Cyber Command's permanent headquarters. Authorities in Louisiana estimated that the facility would bring at least 10,000 direct and ancillary jobs, billions of dollars in contracts, and millions in local spending. Politicians naturally saw the command as an opportunity to boost local economies. Governors pitched their respective states to the secretary of the Air Force, a dozen congressional delegations lobbied for the command, and Louisiana Gov. Bobby Jindal even lobbied President George W. Bush during a meeting on Hurricane Katrina recovery. Many of the 18 states vying for the command offered gifts of land, infrastructure, and tax breaks.

The city of Bossier, Louisiana, proposed a $100 million "Cyber Innovation Center" office complex next to Barksdale Air Force Base and got things rolling by building an $11 million bomb-resistant "cyber fortress," complete with a moat. Yuba City, California, touted its proximity to Silicon Valley. Colorado Springs pointed to the hardened location of Cheyenne Mountain, headquarters for NORAD [North American Aerospace Defense Command]. In Nebraska, the Omaha Development Foundation purchased 136 acres of land just south of Offutt Air Force Base and offered it as a site.

The alarmist scenarios dominating policy discourse may be good for the cybersecurity-industrial complex, but they aren't doing real security any favors.

The Air Force ultimately established Cyber Command HQ at Fort Meade, Maryland, integrated with HQ for the National Security Agency. In the run-up to the announcement, Sen. Barbara Mikulski (D-Md.) proclaimed, "We are at war, we are being attacked, and we are being hacked."

Proposed cybersecurity legislation presents more opportunities for pork spending. The Cybersecurity Act of 2010, proposed by Sens. Jay Rockefeller (D-W. Va.) and Olympia Snowe (R-Maine) called for the creation of regional cybersecurity centers across the country, a cyber scholarship-for-service program, and myriad cybersecurity research and development grants.

Sensible Steps

Before enacting sweeping changes to stop cybersecurity threats, policy makers should clear the air with some simpler steps.

First: Stop the apocalyptic rhetoric. The alarmist scenarios dominating policy discourse may be good for the cybersecurity-industrial complex, but they aren't doing real security any favors.

Second: Declassify evidence relating to cyber threats. Overclassification is a widely acknowledged problem, as the CSIS report and Clarke and Knake's book both acknowledge, and declassification would allow the public to verify the threats rather than blindly trusting self-interested officials.

Third: Disentangle the disparate dangers that have been lumped together under the "cybersecurity" label. This has to be done if anyone is to determine who is best suited to address which threats. In cases of cybercrime and cyberespionage, for instance, private network owners may be best suited and may have the best incentive to protect their own valuable data, information, and reputations.

Only after disentangling the alleged threats can policy makers assess whether a market failure or systemic problem exists in each case. They can then estimate the costs and benefits of regulation and other alternatives, and determine what if anything Washington must do to address the appropriate issues.

7

Internet Pornography
Harms Society

Mary Eberstadt and Mary Ann Laden

Mary Eberstadt is a research fellow at the Hoover Institution. Mary Ann Laden is director of the Sexual Trauma and Psychotherapy Program at the University of Pennsylvania's Center for Cognitive Therapy.

Pornography has existed as long as human civilization, but today, it is nothing like what came before in scope and nature. Internet pornography is ubiquitous and widely accessible and more realistic and hardcore, and its consumption has dramatically risen. These qualities make Internet pornography addictive and visually desensitize viewers to taboo and violent pornographic images. Further, such images harm women by warping expectations of female sexual behavior and increasing the likelihood of adultery. Pornography online also harms children by exposing obscene content to minors and influencing their behaviors and concepts of sex and relationships.

It is commonly observed that the history of pornography extends as far back in time as human civilization itself. Vase imagery from ancient Greece and the painted pornographic scenes at the ancient resort Pompeii are two frequently cited examples, though there are of course many more. The very concepts of "obscenity" and "pornography" have ancient Latin

Mary Eberstadt and Mary Ann Laden, "The Social Costs of Pornography: A Statement of Findings and Recommendations," The Witherspoon Institute, 2010, pp. 8, 13–15, 17–20, 23–24, 27–30. Copyright © 2010 The Witherspoon Institute. All rights reserved. Reproduced by permission.

and Greek etymological roots. No less ancient are prohibitions against pornographic images. These prohibitions have included the consistent condemnation of such material not only in Jewish, Christian, and Muslim moral thought, but also in secular law. Pornography and obscenity have also been traditional objects of preoccupation for legislators and law enforcers in the United States and elsewhere. Two recent, prominent examples of such attempts to grapple with the multifaceted issues of pornography consumption are the 1986 Attorney General's Commission on Pornography, also known as the Meese Report, and the 1987 Report of the Surgeon Generals Workshop on Pornography and Public Health.

Nevertheless, despite the concern that pornography has traditionally raised both inside and outside the government, it is clear based on a variety of measures that today's internet pornography is qualitatively and quantitatively different from any that has come before. This is so for at least three reasons: (1) the ubiquity and accessibility of internet pornography; (2) the qualitative difference in imagery and "hard-core" nature of much of internet pornography; and (3) the sharply increased consumption of internet pornography. . . .

The Reach of Internet Pornography

Unlike at any other time in history, pornography is now available and consumed widely in our society, due in large part to the internet. No one remains untouched by it.

As mentioned . . . , although pornography has existed for millennia, never has it been as widely available or used as it has been in recent years. Though researchers are only beginning to assemble reliable statistics regarding the increase in the consumption of pornography, lay and professional observers have already noted the obvious contribution of internet pornography to that dramatic rise.

Pamela Paul, a *TIME Magazine* reporter whose 2005 book *Pornified* is among the first general-interest, book-length examinations of this subject, said:

> Today, the number of people looking at pornography is staggering. Americans rent upwards of 800 million pornographic videos and DVDs (about one in five of all rented movies is porn), and the 11,000 porn films shot each year far outpaces Hollywood's yearly slate of 400. Four billion dollars a year is spent on video pornography in the United States, more than on football, baseball, and basketball. One in four internet users look at a pornography website in any given month. Men look at pornography online more than they look at any other subject. And 66% of 18–34-year-old men visit a pornographic site every month.

Every second, there are approximately 28,258 internet users viewing pornography.

Paul's observations are echoed in a recent issue of *The Atlantic* by writer Ross Douthat, whose essay "Is Pornography Adultery?" draws attention to the fact that the reach of contemporary pornography is something genuinely new:

> Over the past three decades, the VCR, on-demand cable service, and the internet have completely overhauled the ways in which people interact with porn. . . . Nothing in the long history of erotica compares with the way millions of Americans experience porn today, and our moral intuitions are struggling to catch up.

Numerous statistics drawn from the 2008 Internet Pornography Statistics confirm the impression that pornography is widely accessed by internet users, and that both production and consumption are expanding. Every second, there are approximately 28,258 internet users viewing pornography. Every day, there are approximately 116,000 online searches for child pornography. In 2005, 13,585 hard-core pornographic video/ DVD titles were released in the United States, up from 1,300 titles in 1988. One recent study of undergraduate and graduate students ages eighteen to twenty-six around the country found that 69% of men and 10% of women in this sample viewed pornography more than once a month.

Nor is there room for doubt that this consumption has parallels in the popular culture more broadly. The number of sex scenes in US television, for example, reportedly nearly doubled between 1998 and 2005. Mainstream video games frequently feature pornographic themes; one called "Leisure Suit Larry," for example, features full-on nudity. The game's manufacturers fought to obtain an "M" rating (the equivalent of a film's "R") in order to ensure carriage at Wal-Mart Stores across the country.

Many more examples could be offered, but the point remains: pornography is ubiquitous not only on the internet, but also in many other areas of popular entertainment, including juvenile entertainment. Particularly troubling are the consequences of this ubiquity for children and adolescents. By numerous measures, they are being exposed via the internet in unprecedented numbers to pornographic material—often involuntarily. . . .

Increasingly Realistic, Hard-Core, and Addictive

There is abundant empirical evidence that this pornography is qualitatively different from any that has gone before, in several ways: its ubiquity, the use of increasingly realistic streaming images, and the increasingly "hard-core" character of what is consumed.

Internet pornography is historically unique not only because of its ubiquity but also because of its nature, especially in two respects: (1) its potential addictiveness and (2) its (increasing) realism.

Not all consumers of internet pornography are chronic users, nor are all unable to resist pursuing it to the detriment of other activities. As with tobacco, part of the difficulty in measuring the "harm" of internet pornography is that it does not affect all individuals in the same way. In some cases a casual, sporadic user may be harmed by his pornography habit more than a chronic, daily user. We might also discover that some people are more predisposed toward heavy pornography consumption than are others. These and other areas of research remain to be explored.

Nonetheless, internet pornography does evoke in some users those behaviors that clinical and psychological literature calls "addiction," just as in cases of addiction to alcohol, nicotine, and other substances. The addiction to pornography can even become "compulsive," meaning that it continues despite negative consequences to a person's functioning in his or her work or relationships. As one researcher [A.J. Bridges] has noted, "The negative effects of compulsive use—use that occurred despite negative consequences to the person's occupational or relationship functioning—may be obvious, such as the loss of a job due to surfing adult websites on the company computer, but may be more insidious, such as role disruption that occurs when a husband spends significant portions of his evenings online masturbating to explicit images rather than being with his family."

Although not all of the complexities of the addiction model apply to pornography, the clinical and empirical record shows that to call the chronic consumption of pornography "dependency" or "addiction" is appropriate. To give one example of the addictive behaviors related to pornography, [Bridges notes] "what is considered normal (that is, what the average person does) is skewed for heavy users of pornography in such a way that they are unable to recognize just how uncommon their own behavior may be." Such normalization leads to an "over-estimation of how frequently certain sexual activities are actually practiced," which in turn increases one's willingness to do formerly unconscionable things, as demonstrated in research on adolescent boys. Such behavior was rarely associated with pornography until the internet made the instantaneous acquisition of pornographic images possible at any time.

The peculiar nature of internet pornography makes addiction more likely.

As Douthat noted in *The Atlantic*, "Innovation has piled on innovation, making modern pornography a more immediate, visceral, and personalized experience."

Images that would initially disgust the viewer—including unwanted pop-ups such as child pornography or violent pornographic images encountered during the search for non-violent images—lose their ability to shock and disgust over time.

This increasingly visceral experience has lately been further explained by contemporary advances in neuroscience. One scientist [N. Doidge] describes it as follows:

Pornography is more exciting than satisfying because we have two separate pleasure systems in our brains, one that has to do with exciting pleasure and one with satisfying pleasure. The exciting system relates to the 'appetitive' pleasure that we get imaging something we desire, such as sex or a good meal. Its neurochemistry is largely dopamine-related, and it raises our tension level.

The second pleasure system has to do with the satisfaction, or consummatory pleasure, that attends actually having sex or having that meal, a calming, fulfilling pleasure. Its neurochemistry is based on the release of endorphins, which are related to opiates and give a peaceful, euphoric bliss.

Pornography, by offering an endless harem of sexual objects, hyper-activates the appetitive system. Porn viewers develop new maps in their brains, based on the photos and videos they see. Because it is a use-it-or-lose-it brain, when we develop a map area, we long to keep it activated. Just as our muscles become impatient for exercise if we've been sitting all day, so too our senses hunger to be stimulated. The men at their computers [addicted to] looking at porn [are] uncannily like the rats in the cages of the NIH [National Institutes of Health], pressing the bar to get a shot of dopamine or its equivalent. Though they [don't] know it, they [have] been seduced into pornographic training sessions that [meet] all the conditions required for plastic change of brain maps.

This neurological change is reflected in reports of those who develop pornography addiction or dependence. Based on interviews with over one hundred heterosexual consumers of internet pornography (80% of them male), Pamela Paul observes:

> ... lest pornography get written off as a "women's problem," consider the extensive effects of pornography on the primary users, men. ... Countless men have described to me how, while using pornography, they have lost the ability to relate to or be close to women. They have trouble being turned on by "real" women, and their sex lives with their girlfriends or wives collapse. These are men who seem like regular guys, but who spend hours each week with porn—usually online. And many of them admit they have trouble cutting down their use. They also find themselves seeking out harder and harder pornography.

The combination of hyper-realistic imagery, moving pictures, and rapid-fire bombardment of images appears to mean also that chronic consumers both become visually desensitized, and find themselves viewing depictions they themselves would once have regarded as taboo or off-limits.

This de-sensitization brought on by the barrage of imagery is familiar among therapists. One phenomenon described numerous times at the consultation was the way in which images that would initially disgust the viewer—including unwanted pop-ups such as child pornography or violent pornographic images encountered during the search for non-violent images—lose their ability to shock and disgust over time. . . .

Internet Pornography's Harm to Women

Today's consumption of internet pornography can harm women in particular.

Internet pornography can cause particular harm to women, be they girlfriends or wives of consumers, or consumers themselves. Indeed any woman can be affected, insofar as pornography shapes cultural expectations about female sexual behavior.

Women typically feel betrayal, loss, mistrust, devastation, and anger as a result of the discovery of a partner's pornography use and/or online sexual activity.

By a variety of measures, internet pornography poses particular issues of health and well-being among wives whose husbands are consumers, and among other women involved in a serious, ostensibly monogamous relationship with a consumer.

In North American and Western European culture, wives generally seek marital relationships founded upon mutual respect, honesty, shared power, and romantic love. Pornography as depicted on the internet enshrines the opposite: relationships based on disrespect, detachment, promiscuity, and often abuse. This difference gives rise to unique distress and harm when a wife finds that her husband has been secretly using internet pornography.

Several researchers report that women typically feel betrayal, loss, mistrust, devastation, and anger as a result of the discovery of a partner's pornography use and/or online sexual activity. In addition to the psychic costs of such discovery, there are other harms, among them a markedly increased likelihood of divorce and family break-up. At the November 2003 meeting of the American Academy of Matrimonial Lawyers (comprising the nation's top 1,600 divorce and matrimonial law attorneys), 62% of the 350 attendees said the internet had played a role in divorces they had handled during the last year, and 56% of the divorce cases involved one party having an obsessive interest in pornographic websites.

Finally, wives and other sexual partners of pornography consumers have heightened health risks as a result of the increased likelihood of the consumer's exposure to other partners. One nationally representative study of 531 internet users published in 2004 found that those who had had an extramarital affair were more than three times more likely to have used internet pornography than were internet users who had not had an affair. According to the same study, people who had engaged in paid sex or prostitution were almost four times more likely to have used internet pornography than those who had not engaged in paid sex. Other studies, including experimental research that compares men exposed to pornography in laboratory settings with a control group of men exposed to innocuous situation comedies, also indicate that the consumption of pornography leads men to place less value on sexual fidelity and more value on casual sex; on average, men who are exposed to pornography in a lab setting also become more aggressive compared to men who are exposed to non-sexual material, and this is particularly true for the men who are exposed to the most hard-core sexual imagery. . . .

Internet Pornography's Harm to Children

Today's consumption of internet pornography can harm children in particular.

The few statistics available about the use of pornography by children and adolescents are even more difficult to assess than those concerning adults. Few parents would allow their children to be research subjects in such an area, and researchers do not have reliable access to children and adolescents without their parents' consent.

Nevertheless, there can be no doubt that children and adolescents are far more exposed to pornography via the internet than they ever have been before. One 2004 study by Columbia University, for example, found that 11.5 million teenagers (45%) have friends who regularly view internet pornography and download it. The prevalence of teens with friends who view internet pornography increases with age. Boys are significantly more likely than girls to have friends who view online pornography. In one study, 65% of boys ages 16 and 17 reported that they had friends who regularly viewed and downloaded internet pornography.

An eleven-year-old girl was found creating her own pornographic website, explaining that pornography is considered "cool" among her friends.

Despite the illegality of marketing sexually explicit material to minors, the pornography industry does not effectively deny access to young consumers. Approximately 75% of pornographic websites display visual teasers on the homepages before asking if the viewers are of legal age; only 3% of such websites require proof-of-age before granting access to sexually explicit material, and two-thirds of pornographic websites do not include any adult-content warnings. Nor are there effective filtering systems widely in place on cell phones with internet access or iPods that can transmit "podnography," despite the popularity of such contemporary media among adolescents.

Some of this contact is unsought. In one study funded by the US Congress through the National Center for Missing and Exploited Children, the authors concluded that sexually explicit material on the internet is "very intrusive" and can be inadvertently stumbled upon while searching for other material or when opening e-mail. In a more recent study by the same authors, 34% of adolescents reported being exposed to unwanted sexual content online, a figure that appears to have risen by 9% over the last five years. This 2006 Youth Internet Safety Survey of 1,500 representative youth found that one in seven reported unwanted sexual solicitation, and one in eleven had been harassed online. A 2002 Henry J. Kaiser Family Foundation Report found that 70% of youth ages fifteen to seventeen reported accidentally coming across pornography online, and 23% of those youth said that this happened "very" or "somewhat" often.

Furthermore, such numbers do not even take into account how often young people are exposed to pornographic materials via media other than the internet. Pornography and pornographic references are frequently laced into popular video games, advertisements, television, and music, and also are ubiquitous in music videos. There is also the growing phenomenon of "sexting," or sending pornographic images via text messaging, which is raising unprecedented legal and other issues across the country. The combined effect of these proliferating images and references is that many more young people experience pornography through a variety of media, with consequences that are similarly varied. . . .

Child psychologists report similar experiences and concerns. "Kids today are going to run into pornography online, not erotica," as one Massachusetts psychologist puts it. "They're getting a very bad model. Pornography doesn't show how a real couple negotiates conflict or creates intimacy." She further worries that internet pornography, much of which is "rape-like", is "a brutal way to be introduced to sexuality." The clinical director of Masters and Johnson reports seeing fourteen- and fifteen-year-old boys who are addicted to pornography: "It's awful to see the effect it has on them; at such a young age, to have that kind of sexual problem." A psychologist who runs the Coche Center in Philadelphia describes one case in which an eleven-year-old girl was found creating her own pornographic website, explaining that pornography is considered "cool" among her friends. The Coche psychologist also says that more boys, including pre-adolescents, are being treated for pornography addiction, adding, "Before the internet, I never encountered this."

8

Internet Pornography Benefits Society

Doug Gross

Doug Gross is a producer for CNN and covers technology.

Lacking traditional venues to reach customers, the adult-entertainment industry quietly paves the way in creating or adopting new Internet applications, platforms, and gadgets. Internet pornography was the first online venture to be profitable, and a variety of innovations—from credit-card verification to streaming video—emerged from the sharing and selling of adult content online. Because of their high revenues and customers who are willing to pay for adult entertainment, pornography companies are able to invest in the latest technological advances. However, the possibilities new technologies may bring to pornography are rarely discussed openly.

It was just days after the release of the iPad—Apple's slate computer heralded as a tool for gaming, book and magazine reading and Web consumption—when the announcement arrived.

One of the world's biggest porn companies claimed it had created a way to stream its videos onto the device, skipping the Apple store and its restrictions on salacious content.

The announcement illustrates a widely acknowledged but seldom-spoken truth of the technology world: Whenever there's a new content platform, the adult-entertainment industry is one of the first to adopt it—if they didn't help create it in the first place.

"It's not necessarily that the porn industry comes up with the ideas, but there's a huge difference in any technology between the idea and the successful application," said Jonathan Coopersmith, a professor at Texas A&M University who teaches the history of technology.

"They're kind of the shock troops, and one of the nice things for them is that they can claim, 'Hey, I'm advancing technology.'"

Pornography Is Profitable

While the shadowy nature of the adult-entertainment industry makes exact figures hard to nail down, it's generally acknowledged that porn was the first product to make money on the internet and still rakes in upward of $1 billion annually online.

(Although porn, like many industries, has felt the pinch of the last couple year's recession, leading Hustler's Larry Flynt and others to jokingly ask for a federal bailout).

From the printing press to instant cameras, from pay-per-view to VCRs, pornographers—both professional and private—have been among the quickest to jump on board with newly developed gadgets.

The first public screening of a movie was in 1895. Less than two years later, Coopersmith notes, the first "adult" film was released.

"The classic example is the VCR," said Oliver Marc Hartwich, an economist and senior fellow with Centre for Independent Studies, a conservative Australian think tank. "When it was introduced, Hollywood was nervous because the big studios feared piracy. They were even considering suing the VCR producers.

"Not so the adult industry. They saw it as a big new market and seized the opportunity."

On the internet, streaming video, credit-card verification sites, Web referral rings and video technology like Flash all can be traced back to innovations designed to share, and sell, adult content.

Websites that require memberships, encryption coding, speedier file-sharing technology—all can trace their roots back to the adult industry.

Experts attribute much of the success of AOL, the social networking forbearer of sites like Facebook and Twitter, to its private chat rooms—and anyone who remembers scanning the user-created chats remembers the adults-only nature of many of them.

Websites that require memberships, encryption coding, speedier file-sharing technology—all can trace their roots back to the adult industry.

These days, in addition to the race for the iPad screen, at least a couple of porn flicks are in production using burgeoning 3-D technology. While Hollywood has scored with a few blockbusters, 3-D tech for the television is still in its infancy—and porn, as always, is right there to capitalize.

"Just imagine that you'll be watching it as if you were sitting beside the bed," Hong Kong-based producer Stephen Shiu Jr. said of his movie, "3D Zen and Sex," which is set to begin filming this month [April 2010] with a budget of nearly $4 million. "There will be many close-ups. It will look as if the actresses are only a few centimeters from the audience."

Companies Invest in Technology

For adult-entertainment companies, staying on the cutting edge of technology can be necessary to survive.

Ilan Bunimovitz is the CEO of Private Media Group, the company that announced the iPad porn offering, which uses cloud computing to store a customer's videos.

In effect, he's saying it's like an iTunes for porn—an online service that lets users buy and access a personal collection of adult videos via their iPads. Of course, the slate computer's browser can already be used to surf the internet for adult content.

He said his company, with its 25-member technology department, began working on ways to take advantage of the iPad the day it was announced in January. By the time Apple released the device in early April, the system was ready, he said.

"Every step of the way, when there's a new technology, we explore it," said Bunimovitz. "In the adult business, many times the traditional venues are not available to us, so we have to be innovative to get our content to the consumer.

"With adult content, you need to create your own solutions."

Any new product's pornographic potential remains a dirty little secret—privately discussed by the manufacturer but left unspoken in public.

Porn companies can capitalize on the latest technological advances because of their deep pockets and the relative certainty that their investments will be returned by customers willing to pony up for their product, experts say.

"People are willing to pay a premium for pornography," said Coopersmith, the Texas A&M professor. "You see this with movies, with VCRs—which is when it first really became noticeable. DVDs, computer games, cable TV—if you look at the price of those [adult] products, they're higher profit margins for the vendors."

That fact creates a conundrum for product developers. Often, any new product's pornographic potential remains a dirty little secret—privately discussed by the manufacturer but left unspoken in public.

One of Coopersmith's favorite examples is the early days of instant cameras. Manufacturers were fully aware how many customers would use a camera that didn't require you to go to the local pharmacist to have your film developed, he said.

One of the earliest was Polaroid's provocatively named camera, "The Swinger"—ostensibly so-called because of a strap that let it dangle from the user's wrist.

In a television ad, a young man uses it to photograph a bevy of gyrating, bikini-clad models before eventually picking one to walk off into the sunset—with only the camera between them.

"One of the silent slogans of the porn-tech world is 'Don't ask. Don't tell. Do sell,'" Coopersmith said. "You don't want to be public, but you've got your own private corporate plans."

As for the future, Bunimovitz says he doesn't expect his industry to back away from the cutting edge of technology. He's currently intrigued with the potential of artificial intelligence, which he said one day might simulate a live porn star who could "interact" with the user.

"There's always something new," he said. "At any point in time, we'll be working on new initiatives. Some of them will flop and some of them will be big—but there's always something in the works."

9

Social Networks Are Vulnerable to Crime

Gordon M. Snow

Gordon M. Snow is assistant director of the Federal Bureau of Investigation (FBI).

The proliferation of social networking sites has provided cyber criminals new opportunities and effective ways to exploit Internet users. Con artists and child predators use social engineering to misrepresent themselves on social networks, tricking their victims into sharing passwords and personal information. Fraudsters pose as friends of users, claiming to have been robbed on vacation and requesting emergency wire transfers of cash. And cyber thieves gain entry to online bank accounts in the guise of friendly quizzes on social networks to collect private user information. In response, the FBI works to halt the spread of malware, identify and deter child predators, fight operations targeting intellectual property, and take down organized crime involved in Internet fraud.

Let me begin by acknowledging that the rapid expansion of the Internet has allowed us to learn, to communicate, and to conduct business in ways that were unimaginable 20 years ago. Still, the same technology, to include the surge in the use of social networking sites over the past two years, has given cyber thieves and child predators new, highly effective avenues to take advantage of unsuspecting users. These cyber criminals

Gordon M. Snow, "Statement Before the House Judiciary Subcommittee on Crime, Terrorism, and Homeland Security," July 28, 2010. http://www.fbi.gov. Courtesy of The Federal Bureau of Investigation and The Department of Justice.

are using a variety of schemes to defraud or victimize inno-cent social networking site users, some of which I would like to highlight today.

Social Engineering

Regardless of the social networking site, users continue to be fooled online by persons claiming to be somebody else. Unlike the physical world, individuals can misrepresent everything about themselves while they communicate online, ranging not only from their names and business affiliations (something that is fairly easy to do in-person as well), but extending as well to their gender, age, and location (identifiers that are far more difficult to fake in-person). Years ago, we called these types of people confidence or "con" men. Perhaps as a result of today's high-tech times, con artists are now referred to as being engaged in social engineering. It should come as no sur-prise to learn that the FBI [Federal Bureau of Investigation] is investigating classic investment fraud schemes, such as Ponzi schemes, that are now being carried out in virtual worlds. Other con artists are able to conduct identity theft crimes by misidentifying themselves on social networking sites and then tricking their victims into giving them their account names and passwords as well as other personally identifiable infor-mation.

In addition to identity theft crimes, child predators rou-tinely use social networking sites to locate and communicate with future victims and other pedophiles. In at least one pub-licized case from last year, an individual attempted to extort nude photos of teenage girls after he gained control of their e-mail and social networking accounts. That particular FBI in-vestigation led to an 18-year federal sentence for the offender, reflecting that these crimes are serious and will not be toler-ated.

Fraud Schemes

There are a variety of Internet fraud schemes being used by cyber criminals at any given time. By way of example, a recent fraud scheme involves a cyber criminal gaining access to an unsuspecting user's e-mail account or social networking site. The fraudster, who claims to be the account holder, then sends messages to the user's friends. In the message, the fraudster states that he is on travel and has been robbed of his credit cards, passport, money, and cell phone; and is in need of money immediately. Without realizing that the message is from a criminal, the friends wire money to an overseas account without validating the claim.

Small-scale data mining may also be easy for cyber criminals if social networking site users have not properly guarded their profile or access to sensitive information.

Phishing Scams

Phishing schemes attempt to make Internet users believe that they are receiving e-mail from a trusted source when that is not the case. Phishing attacks on social networking site users come in various formats, including: messages within the social networking site either from strangers or compromised friend accounts; links or videos within a social networking site profile claiming to lead to something harmless that turns out to be harmful; or e-mails sent to users claiming to be from the social networking site itself. Social networking site users fall victim to the schemes due to the higher level of trust typically displayed while using social networking sites. Users often accept into their private sites people that they do not actually know, or sometimes fail altogether to properly set privacy settings on their profile. This gives cyber thieves an advantage when trying to trick their victims through various phishing schemes.

Social networking sites, as well as corporate websites in general, provide criminals with enormous amounts of information to send official looking documents and send them to individual targets who have shown interest in specific subjects. The personal and detailed nature of the information erodes the victim's sense of caution, leading them to open the malicious e-mail. Such e-mail contains an attachment that contains malicious software designed to provide the e-mail's sender with control over the victim's entire computer. Once the malware infection is discovered, it is often too late to protect the data from compromise.

Cyber criminals design advanced malware to act with precision to infect, conceal access, steal or modify data without detection. Coders of advanced malware are patient and have been known to test a network and its users to evaluate defensive responses. Advanced malware may use a "layered" approach to infect and gain elevated privileges on a system. Usually, these types of attacks are bundled with an additional cyber crime tactic, such as social engineering or zero day exploits. In the first phase of a malware infection, a user might receive a spear phishing e-mail that obtains access to the user's information or gains entry into the system under the user's credentials. Once the cyber criminal initiates a connection to the user or system, they can further exploit it using other vectors that may give them deeper access to system resources. In the second phase, the hacker might install a backdoor to establish a persistent presence on the network that can no longer be discovered through the use of anti-virus software or firewalls.

Data Mining

Cyber thieves use data mining on social networking sites as a way to extract sensitive information about their victims. This can be done by criminal actors on either a large or small scale. For example, in a large-scale data mining scheme, a cyber criminal may send out a "getting to know you quiz" to a large list of social networking site users. While the answers to these questions do not appear to be malicious on the surface, they often mimic the same questions that are asked by financial institutions or e-mail account providers when an individual has forgotten their password. Thus, an e-mail address and the answers to the quiz questions can provide the cyber criminal with the tools to enter your bank account, e-mail account, or credit card in order to transfer money or siphon your account. Small-scale data mining may also be easy for cyber criminals if social networking site users have not properly guarded their profile or access to sensitive information. Indeed, some networking applications encourage users to post whether or not they are on vacation, simultaneously letting burglars know when nobody is home.

Some sites provide users with no ability to report abuse, while others either intentionally or unintentionally discourage reporting by requiring users to complete a series of onerous steps every time they want to report abuse.

The Cyber Underground

The impact of cyber crime on individuals and commerce can be substantial, with the consequences ranging from a mere inconvenience to financial ruin. The potential for considerable profits is enticing to young criminals, and has resulted in the creation of a large underground economy known as the cyber underground. The cyber underground is a pervasive market governed by rules and logic that closely mimic those of the legitimate business world, including a unique language, a set of expectations about its members' conduct, and a system of stratification based on knowledge and skill, activities, and reputation.

One of the ways that cyber criminals communicate within the cyber underground is on website forums. It is on these forums that cyber criminals buy and sell login credentials (such as those for e-mail, social networking sites, or financial accounts); where they buy and sell phishing kits, malicious software, access to botnets; and victim social security numbers, credit cards, and other sensitive information. These criminals are increasingly professionalized, organized, and have unique or specialized skills.

In addition, cyber crime is increasingly transnational in nature, with individuals living in different countries around the world working together on the same schemes. In late 2008, an international hacking ring carried out one of the most complicated and organized computer fraud attacks ever conducted. The crime group used sophisticated hacking techniques to compromise the encryption used to protect data on 44 payroll debit cards, and then provided a network of "cashers" to withdraw more than $9 million from over 2,100 ATMs in at least 280 cities worldwide, including cities in the United States, Russia, Ukraine, Estonia, Italy, Hong Kong, Japan and Canada. The $9 million loss occurred within a span of less than 12 hours. The cyber underground facilitates the exchange of cyber crime services, tools, expertise, and resources, which enables this sort of transnational criminal operation to take place across multiple countries.

Beyond Cyber Crime

Apart from the cyber crime consequences associated with social networking sites, valuable information can be inadvertently exposed by military or government personnel via their social networking site profile. In a recently publicized case, an individual created a fake profile on multiple social networking sites posing as an attractive female intelligence analyst and extended friend requests to government contractors, military, and other government personnel. Many of the friend requests were accepted, even though the profile was of a fictitious person. According to press accounts, the deception provided its creator with access to a fair amount of sensitive data, including a picture from a soldier taken on patrol in Afghanistan that contained embedded data identifying his exact location. The person who created the fake social networking sites, when asked what he was trying to prove, responded: "The first thing was the issue of trust and how easily it is given. The second thing was to show how much different information gets leaked out through various networks." He also noted that although some individuals recognized the sites as fake, they had no central place to warn others about the perceived fraud, helping to ensure 300 connections in a month.

This last point is worth expanding upon. Some social networking sites have taken it upon themselves to be model corporate citizens by voluntarily providing functions for users to report acts of abuse. A number of sites have easy to use buttons or links that, with a single click, will send a message to the system administrator alerting them of potentially illegal or abusive content. Unfortunately though, many sites have not followed the lead. Some sites provide users with no ability to report abuse, while others either intentionally or unintentionally discourage reporting by requiring users to complete a series of onerous steps every time they want to report abuse.

FBI's Cyber Mission and Strategic Partnerships

The Department of Justice leads the national effort to prosecute cyber crime, and the FBI, in collaboration with other federal law enforcement agencies, investigates cyber crime. The FBI [Federal Bureau of Investigation]'s cyber crime mission is four-fold: first and foremost, to stop those behind the most serious computer intrusions and the spread of malicious code; second, to identify and thwart online sexual predators who use the Internet to meet and exploit children and to produce, possess, or share child pornography; third, to counteract operations that target U.S. intellectual property, endangering our national security and competitiveness; and fourth, to dismantle national and transnational organized criminal enterprises engaging in Internet fraud. To this end, we have established cyber squads in each of our 56 field offices around the country, with more than 1,000 specially trained agents, analysts, and digital forensic examiners. Still, we can not combat this threat alone.

Some of the best tools in the FBI's arsenal for combating any crime problem are its long-standing partnerships with federal, state, local, and international law enforcement agencies, as well as with the private sector and academia. At the federal level, and by presidential mandate, the FBI leads the National Cyber Investigative Joint Task Force (NCIJTF) as a multi-agency national focal point for coordinating, integrating, and sharing pertinent information related to cyber threat investigations in order to determine the identity, location, intent, motivation, capabilities, alliances, funding, and methodologies of cyber threat groups and individuals. In doing so, the partners of the NCIJTF support the U.S. government's full range of options across all elements of national power.

The FBI also partners closely with not-for-profit organizations, including extensive partnerships with the National White Collar Crime Center (NW3C), in establishing the Internet Crime Complaint Center (IC3), the National Cyber-Forensic and Training Alliance (NCFTA), the InfraGard National Members Alliance in establishing InfraGard, the Financial Services Information Sharing & Analysis Center (FSISAC), and the National Center for Missing and Exploited Children (NCMEC).

Just one recent example of coordination highlights how effective we are when working within these closely established partnerships. Earlier this year, Romanian police and prosecutors conducted one of Romania's largest police actions ever—an investigation of an organized crime group engaged in Internet fraud. The investigation deployed over 700 law enforcement officers who conducted searches at 103 locations, which led to the arrest of 34 people. Over 600 victims of this Romanian crime ring were U.S. citizens. The success in bringing down this group was based in large part on the strength of our partnership with Romanian law enforcement and our domestic federal, state and local partners. Through extensive coordination by the FBI's legal attaché (legat) [office] in Bucharest, the Internet Crime Complaint Center provided the Romanians with over 600 complaints it had compiled from submissions to the www.IC3.gov reporting portal. In addition, and again in close coordination with the FBI's legat, over 45 FBI field offices assisted in the investigation by conducting interviews to obtain victim statements on Romanian complaint forms, and by obtaining police reports and covering other investigative leads within their divisions.

Working closely with others, sharing information, and leveraging all available resources and expertise, the FBI and its partners have made significant strides in combating cyber crime. Clearly, there is more work to be done, but through a coordinated approach we have become more nimble and responsive in our efforts to bring justice to the most egregious offenders.

10

Social Networks Can Be Used to Combat Crime and Terrorism

Economist

The Economist *is a weekly British publication focusing on international politics and business news.*

Companies, law enforcement, and government agencies have begun to analyze data from social networking sites to combat fraud, crime, and terrorism. Financial firms use software to examine social networks and tax records to determine whether an applicant is a risky borrower or fraud risk. Police in Virginia have developed network-analysis software to predict crime and monitor messages on social networks for locations of criminal behavior. In counterterrorism efforts, mapping out the social networks of decentralized terrorist groups can be utilized to identify and trace key individuals. In fact, network analysis has the potential for forecasting attacks and establishing patterns of terrorist activity, and the influence of social networks can be leveraged to promote stability and democracy.

Companies have long mined their data to improve sales and productivity. But broadening data mining to include analysis of social networks makes new things possible. Modelling social relationships is akin to creating an "index of power", says Stephen Borgatti, a network-analysis expert at the University of Kentucky in Lexington. In some companies, e-mails are analysed automatically to help bosses manage their workers. Employees who are often asked for advice may be good candidates for promotion, for example.

Ellen Joyner of SAS, an analytics firm based in Cary, North Carolina, notes that more and more financial firms are using the software to uncover fraud. The latest version of SAS's software identifies risky borrowers by examining their social networks and Internal Revenue Service records, she says. For example, an applicant may be a bad risk, or even a fraudster, if he plans to launch a type of business which has no links to his social network, education, previous business dealings or travel history, which can be pieced together with credit-card records. Ms Joyner says the software can also determine if an applicant has associated with known criminals—perhaps his fiancée has shared an address with a parolee. Some insurers reduce premiums for banks that protect themselves with such software.

Last year [in 2009] an American government body called the Recovery Accountability and Transparency Board (RATB) began using network-analysis software to look for fraud within the $780 billion financial-stimulus programme. In addition to the internet, RATB combs Treasury and law-enforcement databases to uncover "non-obvious relationships", says Earl Devaney, its chairman. The software works very well, he says. It has triggered about 250 ongoing criminal investigations and 400 audits.

Richmond's police have started monitoring Facebook, MySpace and Twitter messages to determine where the rowdiest festivities will be.

Joe Biden, America's vice-president, said in June [2010] that such software would be used to prevent fraud within the government's Medicaid and Medicare health-care schemes. The Army Criminal Investigation Command already sniffs out procurement fraud by scanning text in e-mails. The software, developed by SRA, an American firm, can correlate numbers and phrases written in nine languages with financial databases. If a person discusses a particular Department of Defence payment with an individual not officially linked to the deal, SRA's software may notice it.

Predicting Crime

The police department of Richmond, Virginia, has pioneered the use of network-analysis software to predict crimes. Police officers know that crime increases at certain times, such as on paydays and when there is a full moon. But the software lets them analyse the social networks around suspects, such as dealings with employers, collection agencies and the Department of Motor Vehicles. The goal, according to Stephen Hollifield, the department's technology chief, is to "pull together a complete picture" of suspects and their social circle.

Party plans turn out to be a particularly useful part of this picture. Richmond's police have started monitoring Facebook, MySpace and Twitter messages to determine where the rowdiest festivities will be. On big party nights, the department now saves about $15,000 on overtime pay, because officers are deployed to areas that the software deems ripe for criminal activity. Crime has "dramatically" declined as a result, says Mr Hollifield. Colin Shearer, vice-president of predictive analytics at SPSS, a division of IBM that makes the software in question, says it can largely replace police officers' reliance on "gut feel".

Network analysis also has a useful role to play in counter-terrorism. Terror groups are often decentralised, so mapping their social networks is akin to deciphering "a big spaghetti picture", says Roy Lindelauf of the Royal Dutch Defence Academy, who develops software for intelligence agencies in the Netherlands. It turns out that the key terrorists in a group are often not the leaders, but rather seemingly low-level people, such as drivers and guides, who keep addresses and phone numbers memorised. Such people tend to stand out in network models because of their high level of connectedness. To find them, analysts map "structural signatures" such as short phone calls placed to the same number just before and after an attack, which may indicate that the beginning and end of an operation has been reported.

The capture of Saddam Hussein in 2003 was due in large part to the mapping of the social networks of his former chauffeurs, according to Bob Griffin, the chief executive of i2, a British firm which developed the software used in the manhunt. Senior members of the Iraqi regime were mostly clueless about the whereabouts of the former president, says Mr Griffin, but modelling the social networks of his chauffeurs who had links to rural property eventually led to the discovery of his hideout, on a farm near his hometown of Tikrit.

In relatively closed countries, like Egypt, rapid shifts in social networks can trigger upheaval.

From Social to Societal Networks

Where is network analysis headed? The next step beyond mapping influence between individuals is to map the influences between larger segments of society. A forecasting model developed by Venkatramana Subrahmanian of the University of Maryland does just that. Called SOMA Terror Organization Portal, it analyses a wide range of information about politics, business and society in Lebanon to predict, with surprising accuracy, rocket attacks by the country's Hizbullah militia on Israel.

Attacks tend to increase, for example, as more money from Islamic charities flows into Lebanon. Attacks decrease during election years, particularly as more Hizbullah members run for office and campaign energetically. By the middle of

2010 SOMA was sucking up data from more than 200 sources, many of them newspaper websites. The number of sources will have more than doubled by the end of the year.

Once these societal networks of influence can be accurately mapped, they can be used to promote the spread of particular ideas—those that support stability and democracy, for example. Last year America's army, which jointly funds SOMA with the air force, began disbursing about $80m [million] in five-year research grants for network analysis to promote democracy and national security. An authoritarian government, for instance, may have difficulties slowing the spread of a new idea in a certain medium—say, internet chatter about a book that explains how corruption undermines job creation. Diplomatic services can use this information to help ideas spread. Brian Uzzi of Northwestern University in Evanston, Illinois, who advises intelligence agencies on democracy-promotion analytics, says diplomatic services are mapping the "tipping point" when ideas go mainstream in spite of government repression.

SPADAC, a firm based in McLean, Virginia, performs such analyses on Egypt and other countries in Africa, the Middle East and South-East Asia. Clients include the United States, Mexico and various diplomatic services. Riots, bloody elections and crackdowns, among other things, can be forecast with improving accuracy by crunching data on food production, unemployment, drug busts, home evictions and slum growth detected in satellite images. Mark Dumas, the head of SPADAC, notes that societies with longstanding and strong social and business ties abroad weather change well. In relatively closed countries, like Egypt, rapid shifts in social networks can trigger upheaval, he says. Last year SPADAC's revenue reached $19m; this year it will exceed $27m.

Country analyses have great potential in peacekeeping and counterinsurgency operations, according to Kathleen Carley of Carnegie Mellon University in Pittsburgh. She is developing a societal model of Sudan with a team of about 40 researchers. Foreign aid workers and diplomats frequently stumble in Sudan because they fail to work out which tribal and political leaders they should work with, and how.

Ms Carley's model, known as ORA, analyses a decade of data on such things as weather, land and water disputes, cabinet reshuffles, reactions to corruption, court cases, economic activity and changes in tribal geographic maps. Within the information that emerges are lists of the locals most likely to co-operate with Westerners, with details of the role each would best play. This depth of insight, a demonstration of the power of network analysis today, will only grow.

11

Cyberbullying Is a Serious Problem

Andrew Schrock and danah boyd

Andrew Schrock is a doctoral student at the University of Southern California's Annenberg School for Communication & Journalism; danah boyd is a visiting researcher at Harvard University's Law School, adjunct associate professor at the University of New South Wales, and senior researcher at Microsoft Research.

Cyberbullying and online harassment are difficult to measure; depending on how it is defined, between 4 percent and 46 percent of American youths report being cyberbullied. Such acts are perpetrated with the intent of intimidation, embarrassment, or humiliation. About a third of all reported incidences of cyberbullying involve "distressing harassment," which can lead to depression, anxiety, and negative self-image. Overlap occurs in victimization and cyberbullying, and individuals who both bully and are bullied are especially prone to major psychosocial problems and challenges. Morever, youths who are harassed off-campus are more likely to bring a weapon on-campus and report engaging in problem behaviors, such as truancy, assault, and substance abuse.

It is difficult to measure online harassment and cyberbully-ing because these concepts have no clear and consistent definition. Online harassment or "cyberbullying" has been de-fined as "an overt, intentional act of aggression towards an-other person online" or a "willful and repeated harm inflicted through the use of computers, cell phones, and other elec-tronic devices". They may involve direct (such as chat or text messaging), semipublic (such as posting a harassing message on an e-mail list) or public communications (such as creating a website devoted to making fun of the victim). Outside of academic dialogue and discipline, these two terms are fre-quently used interchangeably, and they have some conceptual similarity. "Cyberstalking" is another term that captures online activities that may be related to harassment, but suffers from a similar lack of conceptual clarity, as definitions of cyberstalk-ing vary widely. Researchers consider it variously as being an attempt to harass or control others online or understand it as an online extension of offline stalking.

These acts are designed to threaten, embarrass, or humili-ate youth. However, cyberbullying frequently lacks characteris-tics of "schoolyard bullying," such as aggression, repetition, and an imbalance of power. Some argue that cyberbullying should narrowly mark those acts of harassment that are con-nected to offline bullying and online harassment should refer to all forms of harassments that take place online, regardless of origin; others argue that online harassment and cyberbully-ing differ because of the element of repeated behavior in the latter, rather than just one instance. These varying conceptual-izations of cyberbullying and Internet harassment likely con-tribute to the wide range (4%–46%) of youth who report it.

However cyberbullying and online harassment are defined, the reach of cyberbullying is thought to be "magnified" be-cause the actual location of bullying may be in the school set-ting or away from it. Online bullies use a number of technologies, such as instant-messenger (IM), text and multimedia messaging on a cell phone, e-mail, social network sites, and other websites. Despite this increased reach, cyberbullying is not reported to occur at higher overall rates than offline bullying. For instance, 67% of teenagers said that bullying happens more offline than online, 54% of grade 7 students were victims of traditional bullying and less than half that number (25%) were victims of cyberbullying, 42% of cyberbully victims were also school bullying victims, and a survey of more than 15,000 students in grades 6–10 found that around 30% were offline bullies or victims. In other cases, individuals unknown or anonymous to the victim are the perpetrators of online harassment.

Though school bullying shows a steep decline, online harassment remains level through the end of high school, and has been shown to persist even in college.

The problem of online harassment of minors is relatively widespread, with 4%–46% of youth reporting being cyberbullied, depending on how it is defined; date and location of data collection; and the time frame under investigation. In the United States, 3% of youth aged 10–17 reported three or more cyberbullying episodes in the last year, and 9% of junior high school students said they had been cyberbullied three or more times. A recently published study based on data collected in Spring 2007 found that 17.3% of middle-school youth had been "cyberbullied" in their lifetime, but that nearly 43% had experienced victimizations that could be defined as cyberbullying. Relatively few students encounter weekly or daily cyberbullying. In Canada, [researcher Tanya] Beran found that 34% of Canadian students in grades 7–9 were cyberbullied once or twice, and 19% reported "a few times," 3% "many times," and only 0.01% were cyberbullied on a daily basis.

Victims of Cyberbullying

About a third of all reports of cyberbullying involve "distressing harassment". Distress stemming from cyberbullying victimization can lead to negative effects similar to offline bullying such as depression, anxiety, and having negative social views of themselves. As [researchers Justin] Patchin and [Sameer] Hinduja describe it, "the negative effects inherent in cyberbullying . . . are not slight or trivial and have the potential to inflict serious psychological, emotional, or social harm". [Researcher Janis] Wolak found that youth (aged 10–17) who were bullied may feel upset (30%), afraid (24%), or embarrassed (22%) and that even the 34% of victims of harassment who were not upset or afraid may experience effects from bullying, such as staying away from the Internet or one particular part of it, being unable to stop thinking about it, feeling jumpy or irritable, or losing interest in things. Similarly, Patchin and Hinduja found that 54% of victims were negatively affected in some way, such as feeling frustrated, angry, or sad. This finding is of concern, because negative emotions are often improperly resolved by adolescents through self-destructive behaviors, interpersonal violence, and various forms of delinquency.

Frequent users of the Internet who talk with strangers online were more likely to report depressive symptoms and those who are bullies, victims, or both were more likely to report major symptoms. Depressive symptoms and loneliness are the most common effects of offline bullying. Other negative school-based effects of online harassment can occur, such as lower grades and absenteeism in school.

Age-related findings are difficult to compare across studies, as researchers alternately collected age with large ranges (such as "older adolescents"), two-year ranges (such as 12–13 years old), exact age (in years), or grade number (which varies between countries and corresponds only loosely with age). Additionally, some studies focused on a very narrow range of youth, and no conclusions could be drawn on age differences. With these caveats, there appears to be a strong correlation between age and likelihood of victimization. Victimization rates were found to be generally lower in early adolescence and higher in mid-adolescence (around ages 14–15). Some studies identified a peak period for online harassment, such as eighth grade or 15 years of age.

Online harassment and offline bullying affect slightly differently aged populations. Reports of online harassment differ slightly from reports of offline bullying declining during middle and high school. The Bureau of Justice Statistics shows a steep decline in offline bullying from seventh to twelfth grades, while online harassment tends to peak later, in eighth grade, and declines only slightly. This finding may be due to the fact that only a minority of online harassment is school-related and in some cases has entirely different dynamics than offline bullying. Though school bullying shows a steep decline, online harassment remains level through the end of high school, and has been shown to persist even in college.

In a recent study, 27% of teenaged girls were found to "cyberbully back" in retaliation for being bullied online.

Reports of gender differences are inconclusive, but generally, girls were more likely to be online harassment victims and more likely to be distressed by being harassed. Girls are more at risk for online harassment, whereas boys are typically more likely to be physically bullied offline. It bears mentioning that the some studies found no difference in gender with respect to percentages of victims of online harassment, although there are clear qualitative differences across gender in the actual *experience* of being cyberbullied and in their emotional response to victimization.

Perpetrators of Cyberbullying

Youth are most often involved with bullying other youth online. Although there are high-profile examples of adults bullying minors, it is not clear how common this is. Wolak et al. found that 73% of known perpetrators were other minors, but it is not clear how many of the remaining who are age 18 and over were young adults or slightly older peers. Other studies suggest that minors are almost exclusively harassed by people of similar age. Between 11%–33% of minors admit to harassing others online. Consistent with offline bullying, online harassers are typically the same age as their victims and half of victims reported that cyberbullies were in their same grade.

In online contexts, perpetrators may be anonymous, but this does not mean that the victims do not know the perpetrators or that the victims are not able to figure out who is harassing them. Between 37%–54% of bullied minors report not knowing the identity of the perpetrator or perpetrators. Wolak et al. found that 44% know the perpetrator offline, but Hinduja and Patchin found that 82% know their perpetrator (and that 41% of all perpetrators were friends or former friends). Hinduja and Patchin suggest that the difference between their data may be a result of shifts in the practice of online harassment.

Mid-adolescents were more likely to be perpetrators and age (ranging from 13–18) was correlated with likelihood to engage in online harassment. Boys were identified as more likely to be online harassers, yet these findings that online harassers are primarily male again conflicts with other research showing that females may increasingly harass online because the forms of harassment common online (shunning, embarrassment, relational aggression, social sabotage) are more similar to their own modes of offline bullying. Some studies did find girls to be more prone to certain types of harassment behavior, such as the spreading of rumors and being distressed by harassment, yet others found no gender difference in perpetrators. Such conflicting results suggest a need for different methodological approaches and measures of harassment that capture the variety of ways bullying can be perpetrated online by both males and females.

Those who are engaged in online harassment but not offline bullying may see the Internet as . . . "a place where they take on a persona that is more aggressive than their in-person personality."

Overlaps in Victimization and Perpetration

Distinguishing between victims and perpetrators can be challenging, because some victims of online harassment may themselves be perpetrators. Though this issue is not well studied, between 3%–12% of youth have been found to be both online harassers and victims of online harassment. Due to methodology issues and anonymity, the rate of overlap is likely much higher. Aggressor-victims experience combinations of risks and are "especially likely to also reveal serious psychosocial challenges, including problem behavior, substance use, depressive symptomatology, and low school commitment". The overlap between online perpetrators and victims shares conceptual similarities to offline "bully-victims" (those who are both bully and are the victims of bullies), a concept reported to include between 6%–15% of U.S. youth. Although these studies conceive of the victim-perpetrator overlap as being related to individual psychosocial qualities, the relationship may also be directly related. The affordances of Internet technology may allow both online and offline victims to retaliate to harassment. In a recent study, 27% of teenaged girls were found to "cyberbully back" in retaliation for being bullied online.

Too little is known about the relationship between online bullies and victims, reciprocal bullying, and cross-medium shifts between bullies and victims. This area requires further examination.

Offline Connections

Studies differ on whether there is a connection between online and offline bully perpetration and victimization, but there is likely a partial overlap. With cyberbullying, bully and victim populations overlap but sometimes involve entirely unknown harassers. The most frequent and simple way to measure offline bullying is whether it was experienced in a school setting (although exact location is difficult to pinpoint, given the various technologies and locations involved). By this measure, less than half of online harassment is related to school bullying, either through location (occurring at school) or peers (offender or target is a fellow student). [Researcher Michele] Ybarra found that 36% of online harassment victims were bullied at school, and 56% of Canadian students in grades 7–9 who were bullied at school were also victims online. In other studies, over half of known bullies (or around 25% of the total number of cyberbullies) were identified as being from school, showing some overlap with school environments. Other studies show connections between online and offline bully perpetration and online and offline bully victimization. Although many studies have not examined whether the perpetrators and victims online are the same as offline, there appears to be a partial overlap, possibly stemming from the very broad definition of the activity. For example, Hinduja and Patchin found that 42% of victims of cyberbullying were also victims of offline bullying, and that 52% of cyberbullies were also offline bullies.

The overlap between offline bullying and online harassment also varies depending on who is reporting the relationship. For instance, 29% of online perpetrators reported harassing a fellow student, while 49% of online victims reported being harassed by a fellow student. Those who are engaged in online harassment but not offline bullying may see the Internet as a "place to assert dominance over others as compensation for being bullied in person" or "a place where they take on a persona that is more aggressive than their in-person personality." Some victims do not know who is bullying them, although many do.

Wherever harassment takes place, the effects can have an impact on school. For example, those bullied outside of school were four times more likely to carry a weapon to school. Moreover, Hinduja and Patchin found that youth who experience cyberbullying are more likely to report participating in problem behaviors offline (as measured by a scale including alcohol and drug use, cheating at school, truancy, assaulting others, damaging property, and carrying a weapon).

12

The Prevalence of Cyberbullying Is Exaggerated

Larry Magid

A technology journalist and Internet safety advocate, Larry Magid is co-director of ConnectSafely.org, founder of SafeKids .com and Safeteens.com, and on the board of the National Center for Missing & Exploited Children.

Recent news stories of cyberbullying suicides are tragic, but they fuel a bullying panic that is unfounded. Cyberbullying is not a normal part of youth. A recent study demonstrates that bullying itself has declined in the past several years—from 22 percent in 2003 to 15 percent in 2008. While statistics on cyberbullying victimization vary, it must be emphasized that 80 percent of teens report that they have never been cyberbullied and 90 percent report that they have never harassed others online. Instead of panicking about cyberbullying, adults are advised to teach young people that bullying is abnormal behavior. Adults have a responsibility to act as role models, especially in politics and the media.

With bullying and cyberbullying in the news, it's easy to assume that it's an epidemic. Fortunately, it's not.

Recent stories in the press about teenage cyberbullying and real-world bullying are sickening. It's hard to know how much cyberbullying contributed to her decision to kill herself, but the case of Phoebe Prince brings tears to my eyes. The South Hadley, Mass., 15-year-old was reportedly the brunt of repeated cruelty at the hands of classmates (six of whom are now facing criminal charges) until she put an end to her life.

There is also the recent cyberbullying case of Alexis Pilkington, a 17-year-old girl from Long Island, N.Y., who committed suicide last month [in March 2010] after being taunted with cruel comments on the Web site FormSpring.me. Some of those comments reportedly even continued after her death.

And there are countless more bullying and cyberbullying cases that don't make headlines. But even though the overwhelming majority of children are able to "survive" being bullied doesn't mean that it's not painful. I still have emotional scars from being bullied when I was a teen.

Cases like these have contributed to what's starting to look like a bullying panic, not unlike the predator panic of a few years ago that caused people to worry (in most cases needlessly) about their children being sexually molested by someone they meet online. Those were great headlines and sound bites for politicians, but the research showed that it just wasn't the case for the vast majority of youth. While it is true that kids are many times more likely to be bullied and cyberbullied than sexually molested by online strangers, we need to put this issue into some perspective. Yes we should be concerned, but there is no cause for panic.

Bullying on the Decline

As prominent as it is, bullying and cyberbullying are not the norm. Most young people want no part of bullying and consider it reprehensible behavior. Depending on what study you read, anywhere from 15 percent to 30 percent of teens say they have experienced some type of bullying or harassment from their peers.

And when it comes to bullying in general, the trend is moving in the right direction. Rather than an epidemic, bullying is actually on the decline. A study published last month in the Archives of Pediatric and Adolescent Medicine found that the percentage of youth (age 2 to 17 years old) reporting physical bullying in the past year went down from 22 percent in 2003 to 15 percent in 2008.

A national study of youth commissioned by the Girl Scouts came to a similar conclusion. Young people are actually more responsible, more involved in their community, and more tolerant of diversity than they were 20 years ago. The survey found that 84 percent of youth said they wouldn't forward an embarrassing e-mail about someone else; 6 percent said they would. That's 6 percent too many but still a relatively small minority.

Not all surveys have the same results. In February [2010], the Cyberbullying Research Center polled 4,000 teenagers from a large U.S. school district and found that 15.9 percent of boys and 25.8 percent of girls reported having been cyberbullied at some point in their life. Among the boys, 7.1 percent said they had been cyberbullied in the last 30 days and 7.9 percent of girls had been victims during that time period. When combining genders, overall 20.7 percent of teens say they've been cyberbullied in their lifetimes with 7.4 percent saying they were cyberbullied in the past 30 days. A survey conducted last year by Cox Communications found that approximately 19 percent of teens say they've been cyberbullied online or via text message and that 10 percent say they've cyberbullied someone else.

The commonly held belief that we are going through an "epidemic" of bullying or cyberbullying is not only inaccurate, but it is contributing to the problem.

Turning Numbers into a Positive

There is no question that there is a problem and I certainly don't want sugarcoat it, but it's also important to look at it from the positive side as well. It's worth pointing out that about 80 percent of teens say they have not been cyberbullied while 90 percent of teens say they haven't cyberbullied other teens.

Posing the issue in the positive is not just a silly math trick—it's actually a strategy that can help reduce bullying or, at least marginalize those who engage in it.

In a paper presented at the 2008 National Conference on the Social Norms Approach, H. Wesley Perkins and David Craig reported on a survey of more than 52,000 students from 78 secondary schools and concluded that "while bullying is substantial, it is not the norm." They went on to say that "the most common (and erroneous) perception, however, is that the majority engage in and support such behavior." The reason that this is an important observation is because, as the researchers found, the "perceptions of bullying behaviors are highly predictive of personal bullying behavior." Even though the "norm is not to bully," only a minority of young people realize that. If kids think that bullying is common or "normal," they are more likely to be bullies.

Based on this research, the commonly held belief that we are going through an "epidemic" of bullying or cyberbullying is not only inaccurate, but it is likely contributing to the problem.

A better strategy is to try to convince young people that bullying is not only wrong and and unacceptable but is abnormal behavior, practiced by a small group of outliers. Taking it a step further, how can we marginalize bullies so that they—not their victims—are seen as losers and how can we enlist young people themselves to stand up against bullying when they see it or hear about it?

Adults as Role Models

Adults need to be good role models. Politicians need to think about this the next time they consider demonizing (as opposed to criticizing) an opponent. Media personalities and talk show hosts need to think about the messages they're giving to children when they engage in name calling. We all need to be aware of comments we make in the presence of children and even people who comment on blogs need to think about the difference between legitimate criticism and derision. Children learn by observing our behavior, and there are plenty of adults who behave like bullies.

Changing behavior isn't easy, but it's not impossible. I've been watching episodes of the TV show Mad Men, which is set in the 1960s when it was acceptable to smoke around other people, ride in cars without seat belts, leave trash everywhere, make derogatory comments about minorities, and treat women as inferior beings. We haven't yet completely eliminated any of those dangerous or antisocial behaviors, but we've come a long way. With concerted effort and national leadership, we can do the same with bullying.

Organizations to Contact

The editors have compiled the following list of organizations concerned with the issues debated in this book. The descriptions are derived from materials provided by the organizations. All have publications or information available for interested readers. The list was compiled on the date of publication of the present volume; names, addresses, phone and fax numbers, and e-mail and Internet addresses may change. Be aware that many organizations take several weeks or longer to respond to inquiries, so allow as much time as possible.

American Civil Liberties Union (ACLU)
125 Broad St., 18th Floor, New York, NY   10004
(888) 567-2258
website: www.aclu.org

Founded in 1920, the ACLU is a nonprofit and nonpartisan organization that focuses on basic freedoms. It is involved in litigation and education on a wide variety of issues related to computer crime, including freedom of expression, Internet filtering, and privacy. The ACLU's website describes current news events, court cases, and legislation pertaining to its issues of interest, and the organization publishes various materials on civil liberties, and a set of handbooks on individual rights.

Berkman Center for Internet and Society
Harvard Law School, 23 Everett St., 2nd Floor
Cambridge, MA   02138
(617) 495-7547 • fax: (617) 495-7641
e-mail: cyber@law.harvard.edu
website: cyber.law.harvard.edu

The Berkman Center for Internet and Society was founded to study cyberspace and contribute to its development. Its primary activities include research and investigation of the boundaries in cyberspace between government, business, commerce, and education, and the relationship of the law to each of these areas. Its website features a monthly newsletter, podcasts, and publications on its topics of interest, which include copyright issues, global innovation, digital learning, spam, and online piracy.

Center for Democracy and Technology (CDT)

1634 I St. NW, #1100, Washington, DC   20006
(202) 637-9800 • fax: (202) 637-0968
website: www.cdt.org

CDT promotes libertarian values such as free expression and privacy in issues involving the use of the Internet and other information technologies. Its website covers the Children's Online Privacy Protection Act and other legislation aimed at keeping young people away from content deemed unsuitable for them, spam, spyware, digital authentication, copyright and online piracy, cyberterrorism, and government surveillance. It also includes news items and descriptions of and comments on current legislation and court cases.

Coalition Against Unsolicited Commercial Email (CAUCE)

PO Box 727, Trumansburg, NY   14886
(303) 800-6345
e-mail: comments@cauce.org
website: www.cauce.org

In 1997, this volunteer organization was formed to address the worldwide problem of spam (unsolicited commercial email). Through grassroots organizing, activism, and political lobbying, CAUCE supports legislative and other actions addressing the reduction or elimination of spam. Its website includes definitions and analysis of spam and its various effects on the Internet and Internet users, as well as press releases, policy papers, recent news, and other related documents.

Computer Professionals for Social Responsibility (CPSR)

2202 N 41st St., Seattle, WA   98103
e-mail: douglas@cpsr.org
website: www.cpsr.org

Founded in 1981, CPSR is a membership organization that works to educate government officials and computer users on issues such as Internet governance, privacy and civil liberties, technology and ethics, and the global information society. Its website includes recent news, press releases, announcements, and other documents. An online action center provides information about upcoming events and activities.

Electronic Frontier Foundation (EFF)

454 Shotwell St., San Francisco, CA   94110
(415) 436-9333
e-mail: information@eff.org
website: www.eff.org

EFF was founded in 1990 in response to an early federal hacker crackdown that threatened free speech by shutting down websites that were not involved in crimes. Since then, the foundation has strongly advocated for privacy protection, public access to encryption technologies, and freedom of expression. It opposes Internet censorship or blocking, which is often proposed in the name of protecting children from pornography, and efforts by the recording industry and other copyright holders to overly restrict the fair use of their products. EFF's website covers related court cases, legislation, and news and includes extensive links.

Electronic Privacy Information Center (EPIC)

1718 Connecticut Ave. NW, Suite 200, Washington, DC   20009
website: epic.org

EPIC, established in 1994, focuses on the need to protect privacy and freedom of expression in the online world, both of which are closely related to cybercrime issues such as spam and e-mail fraud, identity theft, and Internet censorship aimed at protecting copyright holders or shielding children from pornography. Its website offers reports and books, tracking of current legislation and court cases, and news stories. EPIC also offers a bi-weekly publication, *EPIC Alert*, and links to related organizations. A separate site, privacy.org, presents additional news, information, and calls for action.

Federal Bureau of Investigation (FBI)
935 Pennsylvania Ave. NW, Washington, DC   20535
(202) 324-3000
website: www.fbi.gov

The FBI is the chief criminal investigative agency of the US government. Its Cyber Crimes Program handles computer-related offenses such as hacking and system attacks, theft of information, fraud, and online sexual predators. Its Crimes Against Children investigative program and the Innocent Images National Initiative focus on child pornographers. Documents related to these programs can be accessed by typing the name of the program into the search engine on the FBI website.

Federal Trade Commission (FTC)
600 Pennsylvania Ave. NW, Washington, DC   20580
(202) 362-2222
website: www.ftc.gov

This government agency, founded in 1914, regulates business under federal law. One of the jobs of the FTC is to protect consumers from misleading advertising, invasion of privacy, and fraud, including identity theft—whether these crimes involve computers or not. Material on identity theft, e-commerce and the Internet, and privacy can be found on the agency's website under the Consumer Information tab.

Internet Society (ISOC)
International Secretariat, 1775 Wiehle Ave., Suite 102
Reston, VA   20190
(703) 439-2120

e-mail: isoc@isoc.org
website: www.isoc.org

ISOC is a nongovernmental organization with more than 20,000 members in one hundred eighty countries. Its members include groups responsible for the maintenance of the Internet's infrastructure and standards, including the Internet Engineering Task Force and the Internet Architecture Board. ISOC maintains a clearinghouse for Internet information and education. Its website offers an Internet Code of Conduct section, with documents covering topics such as ethics and the Internet, site security, and guidelines for the conduct of Internet service providers.

National Fraud Information Center/Internet Fraud Watch
c/o National Consumers League
1701 K St. NW, Suite 1200, Washington, DC   20006
(202) 835-3323
website: www.fraud.org

The National Consumers League formed the National Fraud Information Center to educate consumers about telemarketing and Internet Fraud. The center's website offers tips on common frauds and scams, including Internet fraud, scams against businesses, and counterfeit drugs (which often are sold over the Internet). Also, it includes an online form for reporting suspected fraud. A separate site, www.phishinginfo.org, focuses specifically on issues related to identity theft.

Privacy International
265 Strand, London   WC2R 1BH
   United Kingdom
+44 (0) 20 8144 3077
e-mail: privacyint@privacy.org
website: www.privacyinternational.org

Privacy International is a nongovernmental organization with members in forty countries around the world. Its primary goal is to promote an international understanding of the importance of protecting individual privacy and personal data. Privacy International's website provides reports, studies, and commentary on current policy and technology issues, and also includes an online archive of information for students and researchers.

Save the Internet

c/o Free Press Action Fund, 40 Main St., Suite 301
Florence, MA   01062
(877) 888-1533
website: www.savetheinternet.com

Save the Internet is a coalition of individuals, organizations, and businesses that work to protect the freedom of expression and fair access to the Internet for everyone. The coalition supports the Internet as a critical tool for economic growth and opposes excessive governmental telecommunications legislation. Its website provides information on concepts such as network neutrality, which it calls "the Internet's First Amendment," recent news, and answers to basic questions about the effect of telecommunications law on the Internet.

US Department of Justice, Criminal Division, Computer Crime and Intellectual Property Section

John C. Keeney Building
10th and Constitution Ave. NW, Suite 600
Washington, DC   20530
website: www.cybercrime.gov

This division of the US Department of Justice coordinates and provides resources for federal prosecution of computer crimes. Its website offers many resources, such as descriptions of policy, cases, guidance, laws, and documents relating to computer crime, intellectual property crime, and computer ethics. Documents available on the site include press releases, speeches, testimony, reports, and manuals.

US Secret Service

Office of Government Liaison and Public Affairs
245 Murray Dr., Building 410, Washington, DC   20223
(202) 406-5708
website: www.secretservice.gov

The US Secret Service historically has been involved in the fight against counterfeiting. Today, the agency also helps to protect computers used in interstate commerce from cyberattacks. The Secret Service investigates financial fraud, identity theft, and other crimes affecting the nation's financial, banking, and telecommunications infrastructure.

Bibliography

Books

Susan W. Brenner *Cybercrime: Criminal Threats from Cyberspace.* Santa Barbara, CA: Praeger, 2010.

Anupam Chander, Lauren Gelman, and Margaret Jane Radin, eds. *Securing Privacy in the Internet Age.* Stanford, CA: Stanford Law Books, 2008.

Nicholas A. Christakis and James H. Fowler *Connected: The Surprising Power of Our Social Networks and How They Shape Our Lives.* New York: Little, Brown, and Company, 2009.

Richard A. Clark and Robert Knake *Cyber War: The Next Threat to National Security and What to Do About It.* New York: Ecco, 2010.

Jack Goldsmith and Tim Wu *Who Controls the Internet?: Illusions of a Borderless World.* New York: Oxford University Press, 2008.

George Higgins *Cybercrime: An Introduction to an Emerging Phenomenon.* New York: McGraw-Hill, 2010.

Sameer Hinduja and Justin W. Patchin *Bullying Beyond the Schoolyard: Preventing and Responding to Cyberbullying.* Thousand Oaks, CA: Corwin Press, 2009.

Thomas A. Jacobs	*Teen Cyberbullying Investigated: Where Do Your Rights End and Consequences Begin?* Minneapolis, MN: Free Spirit Publishing, 2010.
Joseph Menn	*Fatal System Error: The Hunt for the New Crime Lords Who Are Bringing Down the Internet.* New York: PublicAffairs, 2010.
Evgeny Morozov	*The Net Delusion: The Dark Side of Internet Freedom.* New York: PublicAffairs, 2011.
Eli Pariser	*The Filter Bubble: What the Internet Is Hiding from You.* New York: Penguin, 2011.
Kevin Poulsen	*Kingpin: How One Hacker Took Over the Billion-Dollar Cybercrime Underground.* New York: Crown, 2011.
Daniel J. Solove	*The Future of Reputation: Gossip, Rumor, and Privacy on the Internet.* Ann Arbor, MI: Caravan Books, 2007.
Jim Stickley	*The Truth About Identity Theft.* Upper Saddle River, NJ: FT Press, 2009.
David Thorne	*The Internet Is a Playground: Irreverent Correspondences of an Evil Online Genius.* New York: Tarcher, 2011.

Siva Vaidhyanathan   *The Googlization of Everything: (And Why We Should Worry)*. Berkeley, CA: University of California Press, 2011.

Jonathan Zittrain   *The Future of the Internet—And How to Stop It*. New Haven, CT: Yale University Press, 2008.

Periodicals and Internet Sources

Tom Abate   "A Very Unhappy Birthday to Spam, Age 30," *San Francisco Chronicle*, May 3, 2008.

Karen Brooks   "Policing the Use of the Internet by Preteens Is Vital in Today's Virtual World," *Courier-Mail*, October 13, 2010.

Cato Policy Report   "The Underwhelming Threat of Cyberterrorism," January–February 2011.

Stephanie Chen   "Facebook, Twitter Users Beware: Crooks Are a Mouse Click Away," CNN.com, October 19, 2009. www.cnn.com.

Lon S. Cohen   "6 Ways Law Enforcement Uses Social Media to Fight Crime," *Mashable*, March 17, 2010. www.mashable.com.

Computer Weekly   "Is Social Media a Security Problem?" January 25–31, 2011. www.computerweekly.com.

Corinne David-Ferdon and Marci Feldman Hertz	"Electronic Media, Violence, and Adolescents: An Emerging Public Health Problem," *Journal of Adolescent Health*, December 2007.
Christopher Elliot	"In Phishing Scams, Your Friends Get Lost," *Chicago Tribune*, June 14, 2010.
Jan Hoffman	"Online Bullies Pull Schools into the Fray," *New York Times*, June 27, 2010.
Paul Knight	"Too Much of a Bad Thing: Internet Lures Kids into Porn Addiction," *Dallas Observer*, February 18, 2010.
Robert Lemos	"Real-Time Hackers Foil Two-Factor Security," *Technology Review*, September 18, 2009.
James Loy	"The Threat of Cyberterrorism," *World Policy Review*, January 15, 2009.
Wendy Maltz	"Is Porn Bad for You?" *Alternet*, May 23, 2010. www.alternet.org.
Revolution	"Internet Regulation: The Web Gets Rules," February 11, 2011.
Michael Specter	"Damn Spam," *New Yorker*, August 6, 2007.
Susan M. Swearer	"Five Myths About Bullying," *Washington Post*, December 30, 2010.
David Talbot	"Dissent Made Safer," *Technology Review*, May–June 2009.

Dan Tynan   "Thank You, Porn! 12 Ways the Sex
                   Trade Has Changed the Web," *PC
                   World*, December 21, 2008.

John Zogby   "Do Americans Trust Their
                   Machines?" *Forbes*, June 11, 2009.

Index